Peace! Be Still! The Gift of Peace

Peace! Be Still! The Gift of Peace

Ricardo C. Castellanos
and
Allienne R. Becker

iUniverse, Inc.
New York Lincoln Shanghai

Peace! Be Still! The Gift of Peace

iUniverse books may be ordered through booksellers or by contacting:

iUniverse
2021 Pine Lake Road, Suite 100
Lincoln, NE 68512
www.iuniverse.com
1-800-Authors (1-800-288-4677)

ISBN: 0-595-33905-0 (pbk)
ISBN: 0-595-67030-X (cloth)

Printed in the United States of America

The Lord will bless His people with peace.

—Psalm 28:10

I will hear what the Lord God will speak in me, for he will speak peace unto his people, and unto his saints, and unto them that are converted to the heart.

—Psalm 84.9

We dedicate this book to all innocent priests who have suffered persecution from false allegations

Blessed are ye when they shall revile you, and persecute you, and speak all that is evil against you, untruly, for my sake. Be glad and rejoice, for your reward is very great in heaven. For so they persecuted the prophets that were before you. Mt 5:1 1–1 2

Contents

Introduction xi

CHAPTER 1   The Search for Peace 1

CHAPTER 2   Ubi Caritas est. 6

CHAPTER 3   Via Crucis 11

CHAPTER 4   The Armor of God 16

CHAPTER 5   Where God is... .24

CHAPTER 6   The Spirit of Peace .30

CHAPTER 7   Peace at Home. 41

CHAPTER 8   Peace of Mind 47

CHAPTER 9   Peace of Body 52

CHAPTER 10   Peace of Soul 60

CHAPTER 11   Peace from Feelings 65

CHAPTER 12   Peace without Fear 73

CHAPTER 13   Peace without Suffering. 79

CHAPTER 14   Praise Brings Peace 85

CHAPTER 15   The Sacrament of Peace. 92

CHAPTER 16   The Prince of Peace. 122

CHAPTER 17   Prayer Brings Peace 128

CHAPTER 18   Trust in Providence Brings Peace. 135

CHAPTER 19   Heavenly Peace 140
Note 149
Works Cited 151
About the Authors 155

Introduction

"The Lord will bless His people with peace!" This is God's promise in Psalm 28:10. Just what is the peace that He gives us as His special gift? We need to turn to the Holy Scripture to understand exactly what He means by peace. The first promise of peace was given when God made a covenant with Abram the day He promised to give his descendants the land from the Nile to the Euphrates. To Abram, He said: "And you shall go to your fathers in peace, and be buried in a good old age" (Ge 15:15). Not only does this promise mean an end to fighting and war, as in Joshua 9:14, but it also represents the covenant of peace that God has made with His people. "For the mountains shall be moved, and the hills shall tremble, but My mercy shall not depart from you, and the covenant of My peace shall not be moved, said the Lord that has mercy on you" (Is 54:10).

When Israel is promised a Messiah, Isaiah foretells that He will be known as the Prince of Peace, and there will be no end to the peace He will bring (Is 9:6–7). And closely connected to peace is justice. How beautifully and poetically the psalmist expresses the connection. "Mercy and truth have met each other, and justice and peace have kissed" (84:11). The union of justice and peace brings security. "And the work of justice shall be peace, and the service of justice quietness, and security for ever" (Is 32:17). So we see that peace includes security for God's people. God's promises of peace tell us: "And my people shall sit in the beauty of peace and in the tabernacles of confidence, and in wealthy rest" (Is 32:18). God promises that confidence and rest that are rich and satisfying shall come with peace. Peace is described as the blessing of keeping God's commandments: "O that you had hearkened to My commandments: your peace would have been as a river and your justice as the wave" (Is 48:18). The wicked cannot expect to have any peace, for Holy Scripture tells us, that "there is no peace for the wicked" (Is 48:22). "The wicked are like the raging sea, which cannot rest, and the waves thereof cast up dirt and mire" (Is 57:20).

When we teach our children God's ways, they will know great peace (Is 54:13). The Lord promises that His word will be accomplished and do what He wills. Those who keep His commandments and know His peace "shall go out with joy, and be led forth with peace." And the mountains and the hills shall sing praise and the trees will clap their hands. All nature praises our God (Is 55:11–

12). Those who have walked uprightly with God will rest securely in their beds (57:2).

As for Jerusalem, God's holy city—which includes all of us who are in Christ—the Lord says, "Behold I will bring upon her as it were a river of peace, and as an overflowing torrent the glory of the Gentiles (Is 66:12).

Peace represents freedom from conflict and security from all our enemies. It is prosperity to the body and to the soul. The psalmist encourages us to seek peace (34:14), a state of harmony of mind, soul, and body. We must seek it as a gift of God.

From the psalmist we learn much about peace. He writes: "In peace in the selfsame I will sleep, and I will rest, for you, O Lord, singularly have settled me in hope" (Ps 4:9–10). When God infuses our souls with hope in Him, we are filled with peace and are able to sleep and rest, fearing no evil. The psalmist tells us: "The Lord will give strength to his people—the Lord will bless His people with peace" (Ps 28:10). Peace is His gift to His own special people and He delights in the peace of His servants (34.27). To receive it, we need to keep our innocence and have a high regard for justice (36:37). The psalmist explains: "Much peace have they that love your law, and to them there is no stumbling block." However if we are consumed by sin, we will have absolutely no peace (37:4). God dwells in peace, and He speaks peace to His people, to His saints, and to those who are converted to His will (75:3, 84:9).

Very beautifully the prophet Ezekiel expresses the covenant of peace God makes with His people.

> And I will make a covenant of peace with them; it shall be an everlasting covenant with them, and I will establish them, and will multiply them, and will set my sanctuary in the midst of them forever. And my tabernacle shall be with them, and I will be their God, and they shall be my people. And the nations shall know that I am the Lord the sanctifier of Israel, when my sanctuary shall be in the midst of them forever." (Ezk 37:26–28)

Ezekiel's prophecy becomes a reality with the birth of Jesus. Whereas shalom is the word most often used for peace in the Old Testament, and one which is heard everywhere in Israel today, the word for peace in the New Testament is the Greek *eirene*. When one travels in Israel, one is surprised to hear the people greet each other saying, "Shalom." The greeting upon answering the phone is "Shalom, Shalom." On Saturdays it is "Shabbat Shalom, Sabbath peace." It is truly a beautiful custom wishing everyone peace.

In the New Testament we learn that peace, *eirene*, is Christ's gift to His people. Jesus in His priestly discourse says: "Peace I leave with you, My peace I give unto you. Not as the world gives, do I give unto you. Let not your heart be troubled, nor let it be afraid" (Jn 14:27). Then after the resurrection when He appears suddenly in the midst of the apostles, He reassures them saying, "Peace be unto you!" (Jn 20:19). He repeats this greeting when He appears eight days later in their midst when Thomas is also there.

To give us peace is why Jesus came into the world. St. Paul even refers to the gospel as the "gospel of peace" (Ro 10:15), because we are justified by faith and thereby have peace with God through Jesus Christ (Ro 5:1).

The more we understand about peace, the more we realize that it signifies wholeness, completeness, and holiness. Although we can obtain the gift of peace in this life by embracing God and His plan for our happiness, the fullness of peace will not descend upon us until we attain to the resurrection of our bodies and the eternal kingdom Christ has prepared for those who love Him.

"Father God, we sincerely desire to receive Jesus' gift of peace. Holy Spirit, teach us how to do this. We ask this in Jesus' name. We praise You Holy Trinity of Love and glorify You and thank you for Your great glory! You alone are holy! You alone have the words of eternal life. We need Your peace in our hearts and in our homes. We open our minds and hearts to receive it now. Come, Holy Spirit and lead us to Jesus. Jesus, lift us up to the Father and fill us with peace, for we pray in Your holy name. Amen."

1

The Search for Peace

How little peace there is in the world today! Yet, it is what most people seem to desire more than anything else. People desperately need peace. The daily news telecasts speak of fighting and trouble across the face of the earth, as nations strive to obtain justice and the peace that flows from it, so that their citizens may live happy lives. Our cities are ravaged by crime and are anything but peaceful. Family life is destroyed by dissention and quarreling. In their search for peace, some become addicted to drugs and alcohol and live lives of frantic desperation. How *do* we find peace?

In Canto III of "Paradise" of the *Divine Comedy*, Dante wrote with great wisdom: "In His will is our peace," "*E 'n la sua volontade è nostra pace.*" Peace is a fruit of the Holy Spirit and it grows and matures and comes to full fruition in those who do the will of God. If we want peace, we must seek to do His will and pray for His will to be accomplished in our lives. If we are the victims of injustice, however, peace will elude us until the injustice is ended. God never wills injustice, but sometimes we have to suffer it, because of the hardness of heart and the blindness of people with whom we live.

If we are going to do God's will, we must first know what it is. How do we know what God's will is for us and for our lives? Prayer is the key to knowing that. Daily we pray, "Thy will be done on earth as it is in heaven." It is because His will is perfectly done in heaven that heaven is a place of unending peace, justice, love—happiness. By doing His will we make our world a happier place.

So how do we know His will? When we become attuned to the Holy Spirit, He will guide us and lead us to doing His will in all things. Just as He led the children of Israel through the desert with a pillar of fire by night and a pillar of a cloud by day, He will lead us. We won't see the smoke or the fire, but we will feel His guiding Presence in our souls, and we will experience the great peace that comes when we do His will.

For those who are not yet attuned to the inward guidance of the Holy Spirit, there are certain things one can consider to determine if one is doing His will. First and foremost, what we are planning to do must never violate any of the commandments of God or of the Church and it must be rooted in fraternal charity.

If we truly want to have peace of mind, heart, and soul, we will strive to keep the commandments God has given us, not just the letter of them, but the spirit of them. For example, at the beginning of the commandments Yahweh gave Moses, He says: "You shall not have strange gods before me." Just because we do not have pagan idols of stone in our homes does not mean we have kept this commandment. We must not worship wealth, prestige, social position, sex, alcohol, drugs, or anything else. Our Lord Himself expanded upon this text by saying: "You shall love the Lord your God with your whole heart, and with your whole soul, and with your whole mind" (Mt 22:37).

We all know what the ten commandments are: (1) You shall not have strange gods before me; (2) You shall not take the name of the Lord your God in vain; (3) Remember that you keep holy the Sabbath day; (4) Honor your father and your mother; (5) You shall not kill; (6) You shall not commit adultery; (7) You shall not steal; (8) You shall not bear false witness against your neighbor; (9) You shall not covet your neighbor's house; you shall not covet your neighbor's wife, or his manservant, or his maidservant, or his ox, or his ass. (10) You shall not covet...anything that is your neighbor's.

Moral theologians have written volumes interpreting these commandments of God. However, our Lord Jesus Christ simplified them for us, when He answered the Pharisee who was also a doctor of the law that asked Him which is the greatest commandment, by saying:

> You shall love the Lord your God with your whole heart, and with your whole soul, and with your whole mind. This is the greatest and the first commandment. And the second is like to this: You shall love your neighbor as yourself. On these two commandments depend the whole law and the prophets." (Mt 22:35–37)

If we love God the way Jesus says we must, and if we love our neighbor as ourselves, we can do what we want and know that it is pleasing to God. St. Francis de Sales explains this:

> The great Apostle said that *the law* was *not made for the just*: but in truth the just man is not just but insomuch as he has love, and if he have love there is no

need to press him by the rigour of the law, love being the most pressing teacher and solicitor, to urge the heart which it possesses to obey the will and the intention of the beloved. Love is a magistrate who exercises his authority without noise, without pursuivants or sergeants, by that mutual complacency, by which, as we find pleasure in God, so also we desire to please him. Love is the abridgment of all theology." (327)

If we truly take pleasure in God and the things of God, we will desire to please Him faithfully, and, to do so, will try to conform ourselves to His will. We should take our delight in the law of God as did the psalmist. Psalm 118 reveals the love David had for God's commandments. He says: "How sweet are Your words to my palate! More than honey to my mouth (103). Throughout this psalm we find love for God's law expressed. "By Your commandments I have had understanding, therefore have I hated every way of iniquity" (104). "Your word is a lamp to my feet, and a light to my paths (105). "I have sworn and am determined to keep the judgments of Your justice" (106). "Therefore have I loved Your commandments above gold and the topaz" (127). "Much peace have they that love Your law, and to them there is no stumbling block" (165).

If we would find true peace, in addition to loving God's law, we will willingly and lovingly accept His will, as it is revealed to us in the events of daily life as they occur. This is known as conforming to the signified will of God, because the events that occur signify that God's Providence is at work in our lives, and we must accept what happens as His will for us. Often we do not understand why something unpleasant is happening to us, but we know that all things work together for good for those who love God and are called according to His purpose (Ro 8:28). God can take the most dismal circumstances and transform them into something glorious. St. Paul tells us that He is able "to do all things more abundantly than we desire or understand, according to the power that works in us" (Ep 3:20). We should not lose heart or hope when life seems at its lowest ebb. Nothing that has ever happened from the foundation of the world until now can be darker and more dismal that the crucifixion of Jesus. Nothing can rank as abysmal, dreadful, or terrible as deicide. Yet, from this horrible and unthinkable act, Jesus won our salvation and opened the gates of heaven, so that we can partake of the life of the Blessed Trinity. So let us embrace the events of our lives, knowing that God has something wonderful planned for us. St. Paul also tells us that all things work together unto good, for those who love God, and are called to be saints—and that is all of us (Ro 8:28).

God's will is also revealed to us in embracing the evangelical counsels, in so far as they are applicable to our state in life. If we are members of a religious community, then the evangelical counsels determine how we will live and what God's will is for our lives. Many people who are not in religious life have realized the great value of the evangelical counsels and have given much of their wealth to those less fortunate and have embraced chastity.

All of us receive inspirations from God. St. Francis de Sales calls these inspirations "the breath of God." (350) "With regard to the breath of God, it not only warms, but also give a perfect light, His Spirit being an infinite light, whose vital breath is called inspiration, because by it the divine goodness breathes upon us and inspires us with the desires and intentions of His heart" (350). If we would truly find peace, we will keep our minds and hearts always receptive to His inspirations. And when He inspires us to do something, we must do it promptly and cheerfully.

Down through the centuries, the saints of God have responded to the divine inspirations with great generosity. Some have done extraordinary things under the inspiration of the Holy Spirit. St. Colette kissed the face of the leper who was instantly healed of her disease. St. Simeon the Elder, born in 388, adopted strange forms of asceticism. He was only sixteen when he entered a monastery where his austerity was so severe that the others in the monastery decided he was not meant to live in community. His Lenten fasts were extreme, and he made it a practice to remain standing as long as he could. Finally, he had a pillar fifty feet tall built and stood upon it for the rest of his life. People flocked to him and climbed up a ladder to converse with him and receive his advice. Even the Emperor Theodosius and the Empress Eudocia welcomed his counsel. When he was sick, the emperor sent three bishops to plead with him to come down from his pillar, and let the doctors care for him. He refused, putting his health in the hands of God, and he was healed. After spending thirty-six years in the open air on top of his pillar, Simeon died Friday, September 2, 459. For six hundred years, other people followed his example and lived on the top of pillars.

Conforming to the will of God and becoming a saint is anything but boring. Consider St. Philip Neri whose inspirations led him to do many strange things. He walked around Rome with half his beard shaved off. Sometimes he had himself shaved in public with a barber following him around. After he obtained a small dog from one of the cardinals, he would get young aristocratic men who visited him to walk his dog to teach them humility. He received visitors in his room wearing strange garb—a tiny red berretta on his head, a red woolen garment over top of his cassock and reaching down to his knees, while sporting large white shoes. Sometimes he was seen sniffing a large bouquet of broom flowers. His ways of learning and teaching humility were extraordinary. He also shows us that the Lord has a sense of humor. Known as the Apostle of Rome, he is the founder of the Oratory, a congregation of priests that counts John Henry Cardinal Newman among its members.

The inspirations of the Holy Spirit are usually less dramatic than what the saints just mentioned displayed. However, when we know that He is inspiring us to do something, we must do it at once, whatever it might be. When one becomes well-attuned to the operation of the Holy Spirit and is able to perceive His inspirations with sensitivity, we realize that if we do not do what He inspires us to do, He will take away our peace of soul until we do it. He can be like a pillar of cloud by day and a pillar of fire by night, until we follow Him where He is leading us to do His bidding.

Often we do not know exactly what He is asking of us or what the significance of it is. It is only later, after we have accomplished His will, that we can see and understand what we have done for Him. Then we must thank Him in deep humility for permitting us to serve Him and further His kingdom.

In God's will is our peace. The more we conform our lives to His will, the greater our peace will be. The more we deviate from His will, the more anxiety and restlessness we will experience.

So what is God's will? What does He want? Bottom line? The Apostle Paul answers these questions. He "will have all men to be saved and to come to the knowledge of the truth" (I Tm 2:4). And Holy Scripture tells us that Jesus is the truth. Jesus Himself makes it very clear that to know God is eternal life. "Now this is eternal life—that they may know You, the only true God, and Jesus Christ, whom You have sent" (Jn 17:3). It is God's will for us to know Him and to be glorified in Him forever, so that He may be All in all.

"Heavenly Father, we want to know You as Jesus has revealed You to us in His Word. We want to know exactly what Your will is for our lives. Holy Spirit, guide us and show us the way to the Savior. Holy Jesus, You promised that if you be lifted up, You would draw all to Yourself. Draw us, Lord; we want to receive Your gift of peace. Amen."

2

Ubi Caritas est

An old Latin hymn begins with the words *"Ubi Caritas et amor, Deus ibi est."* Where there is charity and love, God is to be found. And we must add, where he has been there is always peace. If we would find peace, we must first experience the love of God. In the previous chapter, we discussed how the first and greatest commandment is to love God with all our being. If we do this, our peace will be great.

How do we proceed to love God and receive His peace into our hearts, minds, and souls? In order to love Him, we must first come to know Him and to realize the great love He has for us. Holy Scripture tells us that we should love Him, because He first loved us (I Jn 4:19). But how do we come to know Him and the love He has for us? The answer is prayer.

Because we have a Great High Priest, Jesus Christ, who lives ever to make intercession for us, and who has made us into a royal priesthood, we are able to draw near to the Heavenly Father in prayer and experience His love. Our Lord Himself directs us how we should pray in the words of the prayer the Church calls the Lord's Prayer, or the Our Father.

The Lord tells us that when we pray we should pray in secret. "But you when you shall pray, enter into your chamber, and having shut the door, pray to your Father in secret, and your Father who sees in secret will repay you (Mt. 6:6). We need to have a prayer chamber, a quiet place where we can be alone to pray to God. It can be anywhere that we are comfortable—our bedroom, the shower, the garden, or perhaps the patio or porch, The main requirement is that it be a quiet place where one can be alone with God and lose one's self in Him.

Our Lord further instructs us not to speak a great deal when we pray. God will not hear us, because we have much to say, and there is no need to keep repeating ourselves. As Our Lord reminds us, our Heavenly Father knows what we need before we even ask. Jesus also tells us that God knows how to give good gifts to His children. We are to ask and then we shall receive. Since no earthly father will give his child a stone, if he asks for bread, or a serpent, if he asks for fish, or a scorpion, if he asks for an egg, we should know that the Heavenly Father will give us much better gifts and give the Spirit to those that ask Him (Lk 11:9–13).

The great gift of God is the Holy Spirit. It is He who makes it possible for us to love God. With the love that He sheds abroad in our hearts, we can love the Heavenly Father with the very love that flows through the heart of the Trinity.

Our prayer is strengthened, if we have someone to pray with us, because Jesus promises that when two or more are gathered in His name, He is in our midst. "For where there are two or three gathered together in My name, there am I in the midst of them" (Mt 18:20). This is a promise that He always keeps. How wonderful it is when we have someone who will unite in prayer and agree with us, for Jesus said that if two of us shall agree, the Heavenly Father will grant our prayer. "Again I say to you, that if two of you shall consent upon earth, concerning anything whatsoever they shall ask, it shall be done to them by my Father who is in heaven" (Mt. 18:19).

When we pray, it is necessary to believe that we will receive what we request. Jesus said: "And in all things whatsoever you shall ask in prayer, believing, you shall receive (Mt 21:22). We must have faith—faith in God, faith in the power of prayer, faith in God's willingness to answer our prayer. We cannot waver or be double minded. The Apostle James expresses our need for being steadfast in prayer in this way: "But let him ask in faith, nothing wavering, for he that wavers is like a wave of the sea, which is moved and carried about by the wind. Therefore, let not that man think that he shall receive anything of the Lord. A double minded man is inconstant in all his ways" (Jm 1: 6–8).

Often we do not know what we should pray for. At these times the Holy Spirit comes to our aid, if we ask His guidance. St. Paul wrote:

> Likewise the Spirit also helps our infirmity. For we know not what we should pray for, as we ought, but the Spirit himself asks for us with unspeakable groanings. And He that searches the hearts knows what the Spirit desires, because He asks for the saints according to God." (Ro 8:26–27)

When we pray with the Holy Spirit, we can be sure we are praying that God's will be accomplished in us.

God has made it easy for us to touch Him with our prayer. He gives us the Holy Spirit to pray within us for what we need. Jesus Himself promises to be with us, if we pray with another believer. And Jesus assures us the Heavenly Father knows how to give good gifts to His children.

The most effective way to pray is to address our prayer to the Heavenly Father in the name of Jesus and in union with the Holy Spirit. This Trinitarian formula is the one that is used by the New Testament writers, and one that will assure us that our prayers are being heard. Jesus has told us that if we ask the Father for anything in His name He will do it. "Because I go to the Father, and whatsoever you shall ask the Father in My name, that will I do, that the Father may be glorified in the Son. If you shall ask me anything in My name, that I will do (Jn 14:13–14). God is glorified when we make our petitions, and He answers them. When we ask Him for the gift of the Holy Spirit, He always answers our prayer. We should become more and more like St. Thomas Aquinas when the Lord asked Him what He wished of Him, and he replied, "Nothing but you, Lord." When we possess Him, we possess everything else.

We are to be solicitous about nothing, but we are to make our petitions known to God together with thanksgiving. (Ph 4:8). We should always make the giving of thanks part of our prayers of petition. We must always thank Him for hearing our prayers and answering them. The Holy Scripture says: "Be nothing solicitous; but in everything, by prayer and supplication, with thanksgiving, let your petitions be made known to God. And the peace of God, which surpasses all understanding, keep your hearts and minds in Christ Jesus" (Ph 4: 5–7). If we are truly solicitous about nothing, and refer everything to God in prayer with thanksgiving, His peace *will* flood our hearts, minds, and souls.

St. Paul also tells us that we must pray with our spirits. It is not enough to pray just with words. Our prayer must arise from our spirit and our understanding. Paul says: "I will pray with the spirit, I will pray also with the understanding; I will sing with the spirit, I will sing also with the understanding" (I Co 14:15). When we sing the hymns of the Church, we should always try to make the words of the hymns our own. The words are but empty phases, if we do not mean what we are singing. If we make the words our own and truly mean them, we join the praise of music to our prayer.

The Scripture also tells us: "Be instant in prayer; watching in it with thanksgiving" (Co 4:2). We are to rejoice always and pray without ceasing (I Tm 5:16–17.) And this is what Jesus tells us—"that we ought always to pray and not to faint" (Lk 18:1). And finally, in all things we are to give thanks. "for this is the will of God in Christ Jesus concerning you all (I Tm 5:18).

In the book of Revelation we have a beautiful depiction of our prayers ascending to God from the hand of an angel.

The four and twenty ancients fell down before the Lamb, having every one of them harps, and golden vials full of odors, which are the prayers of saints. And they sang a new canticle, saying: "Thou art worthy, O Lord, to take the book, and to open the seals thereof, because You were slain, and have redeemed us to God, in Your blood, out of every tribe, and tongue, and people, and nation. And have made us to our God a kingdom and priests, and we shall reign on the earth. (Rv 5: 7–9)

And another angel came, and stood before the altar, having a golden censer; and there was given to him much incense, that he should offer up the prayers of all saints upon the golden altar, which is before the throne of God. And the smoke of the incense of the prayers of the saints ascended up before God from the hand of the angel. And the angel took the censer, and filled it with the fire of the altar, and cast it on the earth, and there were thunders and voices and lightnings, and a great earthquake. (Rv 8:3–5)

In addition to what the New Testament teaches us about prayer, the psalmist contributes greatly to our understanding of it. The Lord hears the prayers of the just (33:16). "The just cried, and the Lord heard them and delivered them out of all their troubles" (33:18). The afflictions of the just are many, but the Lord will deliver them out of them all (33:20). The psalmist tells us that "The Lord is nigh unto them that are of a contrite heart, and he will save the humble of spirit." (33:19). The psalmist assure us that the "angel of the Lord shall encamp round about them that fear Him and shall deliver them (33:8).

Enthusiastically, the psalmist sings the praise of God saying, "I will bless the Lord at all times, His praise shall be always in my mouth" (33: 3). Why is he so joyful and full of praise? Because the Lord heard his prayers and brought him "out of the pit of misery and the mire of dregs" and set his feet upon a rock and directed his steps (39:3). And he will do the same for us, if we love and praise Him and thank Him for His loving kindness toward us.

Many people fail at prayer simply because they do not persevere. When one begins to pray in earnest for the first time in one's life, the prayers, perhaps, do not seem to rise even to the ceiling of our room, much less to God and heaven. It is easy to give up. God does not seem to be listening. We cannot think of the right things to say to Him. There seem to be a thousand distractions running through our minds, taking us away from our prayer. Perhaps we then decide to say an Our Father, a Hail Mary, and a Glory to be the Father and quit. However, if we continue trying to pray, despite the distractions and the feeling that God is not listening, something begins to happen. It might not happen the first day, or the second, or even the fiftieth, but if we persevere in prayer, eventually something will happen. A sense of quietness comes over us. It seems to be almost luminous. We know that in some unanticipated way, God is with us and drawing us to go deeper into prayer.

This prayer of quiet may continue for weeks or even years. We learn that we do not need to say very much to Him, but just rest in the quiet where He seems to be. It is especially easy to develop this prayer of quiet when we pray before the reserved Eucharist. In time, the prayer of quiet becomes like the pillar of cloud the Israelites followed through the Sinai desert, and we pursue it at every prayer time. We begin to realize that we are not alone when we pray, and we find great peace in the luminous quiet that envelops us.

Sometimes when we pray, we cannot experience this prayer of quiet. We are empty and our prayers are lifeless. What do we do? Some people give up on prayer completely. Others pursue prayer more vigorously, undaunted by the apparent emptiness of their hearts. They begin to understand that there is more to prayer than they had ever imagined. Something or Someone seems to be beckoning them on. They begin to search their souls to see if there is something in them that is keeping them from entering into the beautiful prayer of quiet that they had previously experienced. They try hard to keep the commandments of God as perfectly as they can.

The Lord has told us that if we love Him, we will keep his commandments. "If you love me, keep my commandments" (Jn 14:15). The very fact that we are trying to keep His commandments is proof of our love for Him. This will draw Him even closer to us in our prayer, for Jesus has told us: "If any one loves me, he will keep My word, and my Father will love him, and We will come to him, and will make Our abode with him (Jn 14:23). Relying on these promises we should look for Him in our prayer. He will not disappoint us.

"Dear Lord Jesus, we want to find you in our prayer. Fill our souls with the prayer of quiet and illuminate it with Your presence. May You and the Heavenly Father, and the Holy Spirit make your abode within us. We welcome You into our hearts, minds, and souls. You are welcome in our homes and in our lives. Heavenly Father, we thank you for giving us Jesus as our Savior and the Holy Spirit as our guide. Gentle Holy Spirit, guide us and show us the Way—show us Jesus. Amen."

3

Via Crucis

All of us who are in Christ are on a journey. As St. Paul says we are citizens of heaven, but we are not there yet, and heaven is our destination. We must continually push forward on the road that takes us there, for in the spiritual life, if we do not make progress, we fall backwards. The road we travel is the *Via Crucis*—the road that Jesus traveled on the way to Calvary. Our Divine Lord tells each one of us that if we wish to be His disciples, we must deny ourselves daily, take up our cross and follow Him. Jesus tells us that if we want to be His disciples, we have to give up everything and follow Him (Lk 14:28).

We all must walk the *Via Crucis*. If we embrace our crosses, we will find that Jesus can make our trials bearable, even sweet. If we fight against accepting our crosses, they will be bitter and heavy to bear. No one can escape pain and contradiction in this life for very long. They are facts of life. We must imitate Jesus, when life becomes painful, and say to the Heavenly Father with Jesus, "My Father, if it be possible, let this chalice pass from me. Nevertheless, not as I will, but as You will, not my will, but Yours" (Mt 26: 39).

If we want to make progress in prayer and experience the presence of God when we pray, we must faithfully embrace the crosses that are God's will for our lives. We see His will in the events that transpire from day to day. Sometimes our crosses are of our own making. We make mistakes and have to endure the consequences. At other times unhappy circumstances seem to pursue us, and we cannot escape pain and contradiction, because something occurs that we did not cause to happen. Then we embrace the pain, as the signified will of God for our lives. When we do so, we are very pleasing to Him, and He will draw near to us. He is always nearer that breathing and closer than hands and feet, but we are not always aware of His presence. Enduring our crosses in union with Jesus draws us closer to Him and makes us more receptive to His loving presence.

As St. Paul says: "The word of the cross is foolishness to those who perish, but to those who are saved by the blood of Jesus, the cross is the power of God" (I Co

1:18). The Apostle also explains that the sufferings of this life are not even to be compared with the glory that will be revealed in us, when we enter into the fullness of eternal life.

Eternal life began in us with our baptism, and furthermore, Jesus says: "He that believes in Me, has everlasting life" (Jn 6:47). We are already in everlasting life, but we need to undergo purification to possess it fully, for Jesus tells us we must be perfect as the Heavenly Father is perfect. We must be pure in heart, if we are to see God. When we travel the *Via Crucis* our destination is the vision of God—the beatific vision—in which we will see God, as He sees Himself, and love Him as He loves Himself, and share His life for all eternity.

As soon as the spiritual life begins in us, we need to begin purifying ourselves, by avoiding sin and bringing our unruly passions and emotions under control. The Apostle John speaks to us about this:

> Dearly beloved, we are now the sons of God; and it has not yet appeared what we shall be. We know that when He shall appear, we shall be like to Him, because we shall see Him as He is. And every one that has this hope in him sanctifies himself, as He also is holy. (I Jn 3:2–3)

So what do we do? How do we sanctify ourselves? We make use of the sacraments and let the Holy Spirit, the Sanctifier, work in us, as we cooperate with God's grace to purify ourselves. We go to confession after carefully examining our consciences, in order to root out our sins and imperfections. We are not obliged to confess our venial sins, but if we do, we must do so with a very firm determination to overcome them and get them out of our lives. Otherwise, we will make no progress and be confessing the same sins, year in and year out, and continually repeating the same mistakes. If we are really determined to root out our sins, God gives great grace in the sacrament of reconciliation, making it possible for us to do so. He puts His life in us—for that is what grace is—God's life in us. Grace is unmerited favor that is freely given and for which we must always express deep gratitude.

To advance in the spiritual life on the way to the vision of God, it is wise to choose a confessor and visit his confessional on a regular basis, being completely open with him, never dissimulating or trying to justify our sins. We should have the greatest respect for our spiritual father and listen to his advice and counsel carefully. Perhaps we might have to search a bit to find a capable confessor who has the necessary knowledge of the spiritual life and the direction of souls and is able to direct us. But once we have found him, by prayerfully asking the Holy

Spirit for His guidance in locating him, we must not exchange him for another without very good reasons.

We will find that as we begin to work on purifying ourselves, God will give us events in our lives that will serve to purify us passively, by putting crosses in our path. We will encounter contradiction and painful situations, not only in our exterior lives, but in our interior lives as well. Whereas before, our spiritual life was filled with light and consolation, these give way now to darkness and aridity. Our prayers do not seem to rise any higher than the ceiling of our room. We think: "Surely, God is not listening to me." But if we are faithful and keep praying in spite of the spiritual dryness we are experiencing, our souls will become purer, because God Himself is purifying us. Our part is to cooperate, because He is giving us much grace at these times. Spiritual suffering at such times can be great. Mother Teresa of Calcutta experienced years of such purification and aridity, but near the end of her life, it is reported, that the darkness gave way to great light. St. Thérèse, the Little Flower, also endured much spiritual darkness and many passive purifications. When we are enduring such aridity we must be very patient—patient with God—and patient with ourselves.

As long as we are not conscious of any sin weighing upon our souls that would cause us to have spiritual darkness and aridity, we must accept the passive purification as coming from the hand of God and meant to draw us closer to Him. If we persist at prayer, embracing our crosses and valiantly walking the *Via Crucis*, we will eventually come into the light again. We will experience joy unspeakable and full of glory, because the more we grow in prayer and in union with God, the more He reveals Himself to the faithful soul, each time visiting it with greater intimacy and love.

Jesus promises that if we believe in Him, living water shall flow from us (Jn 7:38). Once we have partaken of the living water, we will be satisfied with nothing else. According to St. Thomas, "He who will drink of the living water of grace given by the Savior will no longer desire another, but he will desire this water more abundantly" (*Commentum in Joannem* 4:3).

As we drink of this water, we will grow in love. We must learn to love as Jesus loves. St. Augustine said: "The measure of love is to love without measure." That is the way Jesus loves. His love makes Him completely vulnerable. Because of love, He lets people do all kinds of terrible things to Him—thorns, nails, lance. And He never stops loving. He is love. They try to kill Love, but the more they do that, the more He loves them. They are thoughtless and indifferent, He keeps loving. Love is the cross—love is crucifixion.

People are afraid to love, because deep in their hearts they know that to love they must follow Jesus and go where He goes and do what He does. It means walking the *Via Crucis*. It means having a heavy cross put on our back—a cross that is so heavy that we sometimes fall under the weight of it. It means that when we lift our hand to bless, someone puts a nail through it. Perfect love recoils from pain, but nevertheless stretches forth both hands to receive the nails. And when we try to bring people closer to the Father, they nail our feet so we cannot lead them. And when we love them without measure, they put a lance in our heart.

Some people are tempted to build walls around their hearts to keep people out, so they cannot be hurt by them. This is sad, because when we keep others out, we also keep God out. And we can't live without Him. When we open our arms to embrace someone, we always take the risk that they might stab us. But we who follow Jesus always have to take the risk.

Walking the *Via Crucis* is always painful. Sometimes those who should love us the most are the ones who give us the greatest pain. The Irish poet, Oscar Wilde expresses it this way in the "Ballad of Reading Gaol:"

> And all men kill the thing they love,
> By all let this be heard,
> Some do it with a bitter look,
> Some with a flattering word,
> The coward does it with a kiss,
> The brave man with a sword!

Yes, walking the *Via Crucis* will always be painful. When we love, truly love, we will try to avoid inflicting pain on others—we will try to lighten the crosses they bear—even if it means making our own cross heavier.

Most important of all, if we truly love—if we love like Jesus loves, we will resolve never to do an unloving deed or think an unloving thought. We will counter indifference with more love—greater love. We will be patient. We will bear all things, endure all things, believe all things, and hope all things. We must *become* love, as He is Love. Love will never fail. Love never fails, because Jesus is love, and He never fails. Love is strong as death. Pain, crucifixion, and death last but a moment, but love is eternal. Love lifts us up to the everlasting embrace of the Heavenly Father who will wipe away every tear and soothe and obliterate every pain. And then Love will be All in all. Every pain, every cross endured in this present life will be transformed into a scar of glory, and only love will remain. Let us walk the *Via Crucis* boldly and with courage. Yes, we are fragile and vulnerable, and there will be pain, but the glory that will be revealed in us will far out weigh the pain. In the words of the Apostle John: "Beloved, let us love one another, for God is love!"

"Dear Lord Jesus, we truly want to be your disciples and walk with you the royal way of the cross, because we love You. We will embrace our cross daily and try to keep Your commandments. We desire the living water you have promised to give us. Let it flow abundantly in us, lifting us up to You. We willingly accept the crosses that come to us in our daily life, knowing that they bring us closer to You, and bring You closer to us. Give us Your grace that we may be faithful when life is difficult and we must walk the *Via Crucis*. Strengthen us when our souls seem parched like the desert sand and You seem far away, for we know that if we continue praying, You will make Your face to shine upon us again, when You feel the time is right, and we have learned the lessons of passive purification. We pray in Your name, Lord, and ask the Heavenly Father to hear us as we unite ourselves in prayer to You and the Holy Spirit. Amen."

4

The Armor of God

Holy Scripture tells us that we are to put on the whole armor of God. Why are we to do this? The Word of God answers that question in a very straightforward manner. We must put on the whole armor of God, because "we wrestle not against flesh and blood, but against principalities, against powers, against the rulers of the darkness of this world, against spiritual wickedness in high places (Ep 6:12). Evil is real, and, if we are going to withstand it, we must be armed.

Postmodern man does not want to believe that real evil exists. Desiring to deny its existence, he refuses to think about sin. The Holy Scripture makes it plain from Genesis to Revelation that man and woman are engaged in spiritual combat, and sin is very real. In the Garden of Eden, Adam and Eve were deceived by Satan and led to disobey God. Satan also appears in the book of Job, the oldest book of the Bible. All together the name Satan appears 24 times in just the Old Testament. There are many more references to him in the New Testament.

The name Satan, which in Hebrew means "the accuser," is rendered in Greek by the word "devil." Because he is the enemy of both God and man, he tries to thwart God's plans at every opportunity. Tertullian of Carthage (ca 160–225) and Origen of Alexandria (185–254) also speak of him as Lucifer, because of the Scriptural reference of Isaiah 14:12–15, referring to him:

> How you have fallen from heaven, O Lucifer, who did rise in the morning? How you have fallen to the earth, you who wounded the nations! And you said in your heart: "I will ascend into heaven. I will exalt my throne above the stars of God; I will sit in the mountain of the covenant, in the sides of the north. I will ascend above the height of the clouds. I will be like the Most High. But yet you shall be brought down to hell, into the depth of the pit.

From this and other Scriptural references, Biblical scholars believe that Satan was once an angel of light and a member of one of the highest ranks of angels. In fact, according to St. Gregory the Great (ca 540–604) and St. Thomas Aquinas (ca 1225–1274), among others, he was the chief angel. St. Gregory says he was "set over all the hosts of angels, surpassed them in brightness, and was by comparison the most illustrious among them (Hom. xxxiv in Ev.) St Thomas cites Psalm 103: 26 as referring to Satan. "This dragon that Thou hast formed—He who was more excellent than the rest in nature became the greater in malice." According to St. Thomas, when he fell, Satan took about one third of the angels with him. His basis for this belief that one third fell with him is the scriptural text of Revelation 12: 3 that the dragon drew with him "the third part of the stars of heaven" (I. 63).

Jesus also talks about the defection of Satan, saying that He saw "Satan like lightning falling from heaven" (Lk 10:18). Commenting on this scripture, Origen remarks that it tells us "at one time he was light," that he was, in fact, at one time in heaven. "In this manner, then, did that being once exist as light, before he went astray, and fell to this place, and had his glory turned into dust, which is peculiarly the mark of the wicked" (1: 6).

On this same topic, we read in the book of Revelation the following:

> And there was a great battle in heaven, Michael and his angels fought with the dragon, and the dragon fought and his angels. And they prevailed not, neither was their place found any more in heaven. And that great dragon was cast out, that old serpent, who is called the devil and Satan, who seduces the whole world, and he was cast unto the earth, and his angels were thrown down with him. (7–9)

Why was there a war in heaven? Why was Satan cast out? There has been much speculation by theologians on these questions. Some suggest that when Satan heard that the Second Person of the Trinity was going to become man, born of a woman, he revolted because of his great pride and refused to serve God. St. Anselm of Canterbury (1033–1109), known as Doctor Subtiles, says that he fell because he did not will what he was supposed to will and "unjustly willed what he did not possess and was not supposed to will" (4). Furthermore, in Anselm's view, he did not accept the gift of perseverance that the good angels accepted.

Interestingly St. Bernard of Clairvaux (1090–1153) suggests that Satan set up his will against God, thinking that he could get away with it. He puts the following reasoning in the mind of Satan:

> But surely there is no reason to be afraid? It is true that my wickedness cannot please him, because he is good (Jn 7:12). But would it please him any better to

act badly himself? I should say that even if I should act wrongly in going against his will, he would act wrongly in taking revenge. He cannot want to avenge himself for my sin, for he cannot will to lose his good; nor is he able to." (*Works* 127)

The great deceiver deceived himself. God cast him out of heaven.

"Cast out of heaven," Bernard addresses him, "you cannot stay on the earth. Choose for yourself a place in the air (Ep 2: 2), not able to sit but to hang there, so that you who have tried to shake the stability of eternity may feel the punishment of your own instability."

After Satan's fall there are henceforth two societies of angels. Augustine (354–430), writing about the two societies of angels, observes that the one is "blazing with the holy love of God, the other reeking with the unclear lust of self-advancement."

> And since, as it is written, "God resists the proud, but gives grace unto the humble," we may say, the one dwelling in the heaven of heavens, the other cast thence, and raging through the lower regions of the air; the one tranquil in the brightness of piety, the other tempest-tossed with beclouding desires; the one, at God's pleasure, tender, succoring, justly avenging—the other, set on by its own pride, boiling with the lust of subduing and hurting; the one the minister of God's goodness to the utmost of their good pleasure, the other held in by God's power from doing the harm it would; the former laughing at the latter when it does good unwillingly by its persecutions, the latter envying the former when it gathers in its pilgrims. These two angelic communities, then, dissimilar and contrary to one another, the one both by nature good and by will upright, the other also good by nature but by will depraved. (*City* XI 33)

What is to be the fate of the devil and the angels that followed him? The Apostle Jude says: "And I remind you of those angels who were once pure and holy, but turned to a life of sin. Now God has them chained up in prisons of darkness, waiting for the judgment day" (Jd 6). St. Peter confirms this, saying: "For God did not spare even the angels who sinned, but threw them into hell, chained in gloomy caves and darkness until the judgment day" (II Pe 2:4).

The apostles were well aware that some of the angels of darkness still roam throughout the world seeking the ruin of souls. The Apostle Peter tells us that we must be sober and watch, because our "adversary the devil, as a roaring lion, goes about seeking whom he may devour" (I Pe 5:8). Therefore he directs us to resist the devil. The Apostle James assures us if we resist the devil, he will flee from us (Jm 4:7).

As we read the Gospels, we notice that there are frequent accounts of Jesus encountering the angels of darkness, as they afflict various people. All these accounts demonstrate that Jesus has complete authority over them, and they must obey Him. Obviously, they know who He is, as is shown in His encounter with the possessed man in the synagogue who shouts at Him, "Let us alone, what have we to do with You, Jesus of Nazareth? Have you come to destroy us? I know who you are—the holy one of God" (Lk 4: 33–35).

When Jesus rebukes the devil and commands him to leave, the people marvel at His authority over him. By his frequent encounters with the powers of darkness, Jesus demonstrates that they must obey Him. This can be observed also in His encounter with the devils that possessed two men in the country of the Gerasens (Mt 8:28). Mark records the same event (5:1). After Jesus crossed over into the country of the Gerasens, a man came out of the sepulchers where he lived, because he had an unclean spirit and was so fierce that he broke the chains that people had put on him to restrain him. He was so totally possessed that he took stones and lacerated his flesh. Luke, in his account, records that the man was naked.

When the possessed man saw Jesus in the distance, he ran and adored him, crying, "What have I to do with you, Jesus, the Son of the Most High God? I adjure you by God that you torment me not." Matthew records the devil as saying: "Have you come hither to torment us before the time?" The significant thing is that the devil recognizes Jesus and knows who He is and the authority He has over him. He also knows that a day of judgment will come for him in the future. Matthew quotes Jesus as saying that eternal fire is prepared for the devil and his demons (Mt 25:41). It is also very significant that the devil who says his name is legion—because there are many of them possessing the wild man—requests that they, all of them, be permitted to invade a herd of swine. They cannot do this without the permission of Jesus. They are completely under his power.

Rebelling against God and opposed to Him, Satan tries with his lies to seduce those who follow the Lord. He is a dangerous enemy of every Christian. The book of Revelation speaks to this: "Woe to the earth, and to the sea, because the devil is come down unto you, having great wrath, knowing that he has but a short time" (12:12).

Satan's time is short because Jesus utterly defeated him with His death, resurrection, and ascension. Yet Satan tries to destroy the life of grace in every Christian. He tries to prevent the spread of the kingdom of God, by taking possession of as much of this world as he can. It is normal for Christians to have to struggle against the powers of darkness, as we work to establish the faith of Christ and its standards in this sin-filled world that is ruled largely by people who have aligned themselves with Satan and his values.

There is a web of evil in the world and the influence of Satan is pervasive in our society and in our world. One has only to read the newspapers to verify the truth of this statement. The angels, who fell and followed Satan, when he defected from the service of God, still support him and do his bidding. Not only do they serve him, there are many people and institutions that serve him as well, most of them unwittingly, however. In order to survive the onslaughts of evil that attack us daily, we must do as St. Paul instructs us to do—put on the whole armor of God. Only this "armor of light" will make it possible for us to withstand the attacks of the enemy. We must be wise, "redeeming the time, because the days are evil" (Ep 5:16).

What is the armor of God? It is the protection God has devised for us to use in overcoming the attacks of Satan. Since we are engaged in spiritual combat with the powers of darkness, we need spiritual armor to defeat them. We must first gird ourselves with the truth. Satan is a deceiver and a liar who cannot endure the truth that always sets the believer free. Christ is the truth as He proclaims in John 14:6: "I am the way, and the truth, and the life." As St. Paul directs us, we "must put on the Lord Jesus Christ" (Ro 13:14). Satan and his dark angels are far more powerful and cunning than we are, and we can only triumph over them, if we live in Christ and His life abides in us. "Stand therefore," Paul instructs us, "having your loins girt about with truth, and having on the breastplate of righteousness" (Ep 6:14). Alone, we cannot stand against the deceits of the devil; we need the whole armor of God.

What is the breastplate of righteousness? It is a pure conscience. The snares of the evil one cannot trap anyone who is enveloped in truth and has a clear con-science. We must always try very hard to avoid all sin, and if we are aware of any sin, confess it at once. The soul in a state of grace is powerful against the attacks of the evil one.

The armor of God also calls for our being "shod with the preparation of the gospel of peace" (Ep 6:15). We must be people of peace and walk in the ways of the gospel of peace. Our hearts must be at peace and all unruly desires put to rest. Anger, pride, envy, lust, avarice, greed, and sloth must find no dwelling place within us. For in them the devil can build strongholds used to attack us. As St. Paul says, we must give the devil no room (Ep 4:27).

Faith is our shield. With it we can extinguish "all the fiery darts of the wicked one." When Paul wrote the epistle to the Ephesians, he was living in Rome and was aware of the armor of the Roman soldier whose shield was four feet tall and two and a half feet wide and covered the man's entire trunk. Since it was the custom of the enemy to shoot fiery darts at the soldiers, they were well equipped with these shields to keep them from harming them. The shields were especially effective when the soldiers would stand side by side so that their shields were joined together, making an impenetrable wall. We the soldiers of Christ also need solidarity in faith to keep out the fiery darts of the enemy. The fiery darts symbolize many things—heresies and attacks on the passions, among other things. The shield of faith will protect us and keep us safe during the battle with the enemy.

Since the head is the most vulnerable part of the human body, we are directed to wear the helmet of salvation. Our minds are filled with thoughts of Jesus and what He has done to save us. We are His people, and He has triumphed over the devil, and He will give us the power to do likewise.

All these parts of the armor of God are meant to protect us, when we are on the defensive. We also need offensive weapons. Chief among these is the sword of the Spirit—the Word of God. We must keep the words of the Scripture ever in our minds and hearts. We must pray in the Spirit at all times "with all instance and supplication for all the saints." We need to pray for the Church—her priests, her sheep, and the little lambs in Christ. With Spirit filled prayer, we can defeat the fieriest attacks of the enemy.

We must always keep in mind that warfare against the devil is normal in the Christian life. We must always struggle to make our lives reflect the values of the kingdom of God, while we live in this material world that is under the influence of Satan. The powers of darkness are not able to work directly upon our wills or our intellects. They can, however, operate upon our imagination, memory, and our senses. And by attacking them, they can influence our wills indirectly. We are not to worry about this, because St. Paul tells us that the forces of evil will not be allowed to tempt us more than we can manage, for God always provides a way of escape from the temptations (I Co 10:13). However, all temptation does not come from the devil.

How can we recognize diabolical temptation? We can recognize it by its severity, the suddenness with which it attacks us, the length of time it endures, and the way it fills the soul with turmoil and tries to get us to do strange things.

What do we do, if we believe we are experiencing a diabolical temptation? Blessed salt and holy water and the things used by the saints who have fought such temptations.

If we are trying to serve God, we will be tempted. According to St. Jean Marie Vianney, the Curé of Ars, sorely tried by the devil who even shook his bed while he was in it:

The greatest saints are those who have been tempted the most. If Our Lord was tempted, it was in order to show us that we must be also. It follows, therefore, that we must expect temptation. If you ask me what is the cause of our temptations, I shall tell you that it is the beauty and the great worth and importance of our souls which the Devil values and which he loves so much that he would consent to suffer two Hells, if necessary, if by so doing he could drag our souls into Hell.

St. Cyril of Jerusalem (315–386) advised converts to the Catholic Church about the attacks of the evil one in his catechetical lectures given in the third century. His advice is well given.

The unclean devil, when he comes upon a man's soul (may the Lord deliver from him every soul of those who hear me, and of those who are not present), he comes like a wolf upon a sheep, ravening for blood, and ready to devour. His coming is most fierce; the sense of it most oppressive; the mind becomes darkened; his attack is an injustice also, and so is his usurpation of another's possession. For he makes forcible use of another's body, and another's instruments, as if they were his own; he throws down him who stands upright (for he is akin to him who fell from heaven; he twists the tongue and distorts the lips; foam comes instead of words; the man is filled with darkness; his eye is open, yet the soul sees not through it; and the miserable man gasps convulsively at the point of death. The devils are verily foes of men, using them foully and mercilessly. (16.15)

Although the attacks of the evil one are great, Cyril insists that we are not to fear, because in the power of the Holy Spirit we can overcome them all.

A mighty ally and protector, therefore, have we from God—a great Teacher of the Church, a mighty Champion on our behalf. Let us not be afraid of the demons, nor of the devil, for mightier is He who fights for us. Only let us open to Him our doors; for He goes about seeking such as are worthy and searching on whom He may confer His gifts. (16.19)

We must always remember that the devil is a defeated foe. Jesus triumphed over him with His death on the cross, His powerful resurrection, and glorious ascension into heaven, where He lives ever to make intercession for us as our great High Priest. Even the devil must bow before Him, as St. Paul says, at the name of Jesus every knee must bow and every tongue confess that He is Lord to the glory of God the Father (Ro 14:11, Ph 2:10). Satan can deceive us, only if we permit him to do so.

While Satan thinks he possesses the world, he is mistaken. God is the owner of everything that exists. The only thing the devil possesses is his freedom and he will lose that, when he and those that follow him are cast into the pit of hell. And we know that hell exists, and that he is destined to go there, because Jesus tells us that it is so.

Satan is not an anti-Christ. Rather he is a false god whose power is very limited and temporary. St. Paul refers to him as "the god of this world" and says that he "has blinded the minds of unbelievers that the light of the gospel of the glory of Christ, who is the image of God, should not shine unto them." (II Co 4:4). Nevertheless, we need not fear him, for as the Apostle James says, we are to be subject to God, and, if we resist the devil, he will flee from us (Jm 4:7).

We are the children of God and as such are called to be peacemakers. As our Lord is the Prince of Peace who came into the world to bring peace, we must be like Him. To be truly happy we must be peacemakers and live peacefully with all men. We must try to promote peace, even as the devil tries to promote division. Let us bring peace to troubled hearts and minds. Let us try to bring peace to those in conflict. Let us by our lives and what we say bring people to reconciliation with God.

We must always try to preserve peace and never break it. When peace is broken, we must hasten to try to restore it. The God we serve is a God of peace (Heb 13:20). Over and over again, the Holy Scripture tells us to be at peace with one another. We are to "follow peace with all men, and holiness without which no man shall see God" Heb (12:14). St Paul writes in Philippians: "Fulfill my joy that you may be of one mind, having the same charity, being of one accord, agreeing in sentiment" (2:2).

Discord is of the devil and one of the best ways to defeat his plans is to abide in peace. As the Psalmist says: "Let peace be in your strength" (Ps 121:7). We will also find our strength in peace.

As we follow the Prince of Peace, our Lord Jesus Christ, he will free us from the attacks of the evil one, so that free from everything that would harm us, we can adore and worship the God of Peace in the peace of our souls.

"Lord Jesus, we thank you that you have overcome Satan and all his deceptions. Show us also how to overcome him and to be more than conquerors by donning the whole armor of God that You have provided for us and by letting the Spirit of Peace dwell in us. When we are tempted, let us always fly to You for protection, knowing that You will always provide a way of escape for us. Amen."

5

Where God is...

An old saying has it that where God is there is love and where He has been there is peace. There is much wisdom expressed in this saying. Anyone who wishes to find peace should seek to grow in love, because as we grow in love our peace becomes deeper and deeper. There are degrees in loving God. We have all heard that we are to do unto others, as we would have them do unto us (Mt 7:12). This is the degree of love that beginners demonstrate. The Holy Scriptures says: "All things therefore whatsoever you would that men should do to you, do you also to them" (Mt 7:12).

People who want to grow in love may advance to the second degree, which is expressed in Jesus' response to the Pharisee, a doctor of the law, who, in an attempt to bait Him, asked, "Master, which is the greatest commandment in the law?" (Mt 22:36) Jesus answered him saying, "You shall love the Lord your God with your whole heart, and with your whole soul, and with your whole mind. This is the greatest and the first commandment, and the second is like to this: You shall love your neighbor as yourself" (Mt 22:37–39).

In pursuing the second degree of love, we must first learn to love ourselves, if we are going to love others. If we hate ourselves, it is impossible to love others, as we love ourselves. Unfortunately, many people do hate themselves, and for that reason are incapable of growing in love and will not be able to reach the third degree of love.

Jesus speaking of the greatest love says: "A new commandment I give unto you: That you love one another, as I have loved you, that you also love one another" (Jn 13:34). We are to love each other the way He has loved us. This means we are not to measure our love, but rather to love without measure, sacrificing ourselves for those we love. Expanding on this, Jesus explains. "Greater love than this no man has, that a man lay down his life for his friends" (Jn 15:13). He then immediately adds, "You are my friends, if you do the things that I command you. I will not now call you servants, for the servant knows not what his lord does. But I have called you friends, because all things whatsoever I have heard of my Father, I have made known to you" (Jn 15:14–15). "These things I command you, that you love one another" (Jn 15:17).

We must remark here that such love—that we love others as Jesus has loved us—is not an option, but it is a commandment. Speaking of how important it is that we keep this commandment, Pope John Paul II said in a homily he preached in San Antonio, Texas on September 13, 1987 the following:

> We die in the physical body when all the energies of life are extinguished. We die through sin when love dies in us. Outside of love there is no life. If man opposes love and lives without love, death takes its root in his soul and grows. For this reason Christ cries out: "I give you a new commandment: Love one another. Such as my love has been for you so must your love be for each other" (Jn 13:34). The cry for love is the cry for life, for the victory of the soul over sin and death. The source of this victory is the Cross of Jesus Christ: His Death and His Resurrection."

In giving us this new commandment, Jesus calls us friends and then defines friendship as an intimate communication, explaining that He has revealed to us all that His Father has told Him. There are many loves in our lives—love of country, parents, family, spouse, children, among others. In each kind of love there are certain elements that set it apart from other loves. The love of friendship is characterized by the sharing of the most intimate and secret thoughts and feeling of our beings. Jesus reveals to us that the plan of life for a Christian consists in becoming a true friend of His. We are to receive the friendship of Jesus Christ and respond to it. Just as Jesus reveals Himself to us and the most intimate things the Father reveals to Him, we are to confide completely in Him and follow His way and live in constant true friendship with Him.

The whole of Christian life is love. It is found in embracing Christ's new commandment and understanding why Jesus gives it to us, because it is important to realize the reason Jesus gives us this new commandment. He explains this. "These things I have spoken to you, that My joy may be in you, and your joy may be filled" (Jn 15:11). Again He says: "This is my commandment, that you love one another, as I have loved you" (Jn 15:12).

This commandment is the key to happiness in the life of every human being, because life is only deeply experienced when we love. The saddest thing in life is to live without love. Consider this. If you have a baby and feed and clothe him and do not love him and give him tender loving care, he will develop into an abnormal person. Love is as important as food. The whole life of a human being, of a Christian, is to train us how to live in love and how to prepare us for the next life, for the life of heaven is participating and enjoying perfect and total love for all eternity.

As we grow in love, this is what happens. We pass from egoism to oblation. We go from being self-centered to being concerned more with others than we are with ourselves. Our human inclination is to live on a natural level in which our bodies have a tendency to fight anything that opposes them. For example, if you transplant a kidney, the body tries to reject it, in an attempt to destroy anything that is foreign to it. This is the law we live by.

When we are born, we are egotists. A newborn baby makes himself king of the house. It matters not to him if it is two in the morning or two in the afternoon. If he wants something, he lets everyone know about it, and his wants must be satisfied. He controls the entire family. To reach the third degree of love, we must go from this state of egoism to a state of oblation—of self-giving. There is no greater joy than to live in perfect love, sacrificing oneself for those we love, accepting their love in return for ours.

Jesus' command to love does not say, "When you love people, it does not matter, if they love you in return." People who think this are terribly deceived. Some people say, "O, I love, and I don't care whether they love me in return or not. If people do not respond to my love, it makes no difference to me." Such a person is greatly mistaken. It *is* important to us, if people respond to our love or not. Jesus says love one another, and that means that love must be reciprocated. Love that is not reciprocated is a frustrated love. We Christians must love in such a manner that those we love *will* respond to our love with love.

The ancient world was amazed when they saw how Christians loved one another and demonstrated that love. "See how they love one another!" was commonly remarked. Today we hear a lot about "tough love" and love residing in the will and being a decision to do good to the one we love. That great Doctor of the Church, St. Francis de Sales wrote much about love. To him love is tender and effusive. He defines love in this way: "Love then, to speak distinctly and precisely, is no other thing than the movement, effusion and advancement of the heart towards good." Since it is an effusion, it is an unrestrained outpouring of feeling. St. Francis de Sales is not a cold ascetic, but a very warmhearted and loving person who believes in demonstrative love. He writes:

> At all times and amongst the most saintly men the world has had, the kiss has been a sign of love and affection, and such use was universally made of it amongst the ancient Christians as the great St. Paul testifies, when, writing to

the Romans and Corinthians he says, *Salute one another in a holy kiss.* And as many declare, Judas in betraying Our Savior made use of a kiss to manifest him, because this divine Savior was accustomed to kiss his disciples when he met them; and not only his disciples, but even little children, whom he took lovingly in his arms, as he did him, by whose example he so solemnly invited his disciples to the love of their neighbor. (38)

Speaking of the love of neighbor in friendship, St. Francis de Sales says "friends must love one another, know that they love one another, and have communication, intimacy and familiarity with one another" (51–52). In this way they fulfill the commandment to love one another, as Jesus has loved us.

How we feel in our hearts is made known to others by the signals we constantly give off. How we talk, act, smile, how we do everything is a signal to others about our thoughts and feelings. Everyone we come in contact with is responding to the signals we give off. Some people complain about the way others act without realizing that we cause everything that happens to us in our human relationships. We are not having bad luck when things go wrong. Instead we have lacked discernment and have given off the wrong signals to others. Sometimes we enter into relationships that we never should have. For example, a woman says she has a fiancé that drinks too much and that she believes that if she marries him, he will quit drinking. This is poor discernment and she is entering into a relationship that will fail. Matrimony will not cure his problem. What will cure it is making a decision to follow Christ and put alcohol out of his life.

It is well for us to know that when we find a defect in someone that bothers us, it is usually a defect that we also have, and we will realize that, if we look into our own hearts. In general, what we have within us is a reflection of what is outside and around us. The friendships we have reflect what we are. We know what people are by the company they keep. Or quite simply put—birds of a feather flock together. Ultimately, we bear the responsibility for all that happens to us—for the good and for the bad. From the signals we give off, we get the kind of life and relationships we want.

In giving off signals, we must not deprecate ourselves. Negative comment about ourselves will make people perceive us in the wrong light and reflect the wrong attitudes on our part. We must also be careful of what we say to children, because they will believe the negative things we say to and about them. We have to get rid of all negative and ugly convictions about ourselves and our children, if we are to enter the light of Jesus Christ and become lovable.

We must be lovable, if we want people to love us. To be lovable we must possess love in our souls. The Holy Scripture tells us what love is like and the necessity for us to love. St. Paul says that if we do not love, we are nothing, even though we have faith that can move mountains and know all mysteries. If we give all our goods to feed the poor and are even martyred for the faith and do not have love in our hearts, it is worth nothing. Absolutely nothing!

Love is patient, kind, never envies, thinks no evil, is not proud, is not self-seeking, and is not provoked to anger and rejoices in the truth. When we love, we bear and endure whatever happens in a relationship, believing in the good of the one we love, and hoping always for the best. Love never fails for God is love, and He cannot fail.

We fail sometimes in our relationships and lose our peace because of it. We fail when we try to control those we love and take away their freedom. Trying to possess those we love will make us very unlovable and cause those we love to flee from us, destroying the relationship. Manipulation is another sin against love that will destroy a relationship.

For a relationship to last forever, both parties must be free. God created us free, so that we would be capable of loving Him and each other. Love demands freedom. Without freedom, there can be no love. It simply cannot exist. Without freedom, there is domination by one person in the relationship of the other. When domination enters a relationship, love dies.

This is true also of the parent child relationship. When our children grow up, we must set them free. They might leave us for a time, but if we set them free, they will return to us and our relationship will be stronger, because of the freedom we have given them.

We must not give our freedom over to anyone. We must not let anyone control our lives, except Jesus Christ, and we should confide our lives completely into His hands. If we let those we love control our lives, we are headed for bitterness and the destruction of love. If we want to continue loving people and having them love us in return, we must cultivate love and being lovable, and we must live by principles, not emotions. If we love those who also love God, we can be sure that they also love freedom, as much as we do, because those who love God love freedom.

We must never take love for granted. We must work constantly to keep love alive and growing. There are those who are afraid to love and who build walls around their hearts to keep people out. They do not realize that by building such walls, they not only keep people out of their hearts, they prevent the Lord from coming into them. The Scripture teaches us that perfect love casts out all fear. This does not mean that we are no longer immune to pain, but rather that we stretch forth our hands to receive the nails that we might receive from loving others. Whenever we open our arms to embrace someone, we take the risk that they might stab us. However, we who follow Jesus must always take the risk. When our love is reciprocated with love, we rejoice that we did, in fact, take the risk of loving someone.

The greatest happiness on earth is being able to love and to be loved in return. We need to give constant reassurance to those we love that they are secure in our love, that we will never leave them or forsake them, just as Jesus assures us of His eternal love for us, because as Pope John Paul II says, "Outside of love there is no life."

St John of the Cross says that at the end of life we will be judged on love. "In the evening of our life we shall be judged on our love for God and neighbor." The amount of love in our souls when we die will determine our beatitude for eternity—how fully we shall behold the vision of God. As St. Augustine says: "God is the goal of our desires. He is the one whom we shall see without end, whom we shall love without weariness, whom we shall glorify forever without fatigue" (*City* II 30:1).

We conclude this chapter with the words of our Lord Jesus Christ: "These things I have spoken to you, that my joy may be in you, and your joy may be filled. This is my commandment, that you love one another, as I have loved you" (Jn 15:11–12).

"Heavenly Father, we deeply desire the fullness of joy that Jesus promises to those who love one another. Lord Jesus, we will not build walls around our hearts to keep out love, because we are afraid to take the risk of loving. Rather, we embrace your new commandment that we love one another, as you have loved us. Holy Spirit, fill our hearts with love that we may love our friends in Christ. Guide us in love so that we may "all come in the unity of the faith, and of the knowledge of the Son of God, unto a perfect man, unto the measure of the stature of the fullness of Christ" (Ep 4:13). Perfect love in our souls so that when we leave this world and receive the Light of Glory, we will be caught up in eternal beatitude with your saints in the great embrace of love and joy that never ends. Amen."

6

The Spirit of Peace

God is a Trinity of Persons. Although this is a principal dogma of our faith, too often we seem to forget it. We pray to the Heavenly Father in the words our Lord gave us in the Lord's Prayer. We meditate on the life of Jesus, when we say the rosary. However, the Holy Spirit is often neglected; we hardly ever speak of Him, except when we bless ourselves in the name of the Father, the Son, and the Holy Spirit. Yet, if we would know true peace we must turn to the Holy Spirit, for one of the fruits of the Spirit is peace (Ga 23:23). Let us look for Him in the Scriptures and in the Church.

At the very beginning of the book of Genesis we read: "In the beginning God created heaven, and earth. And the earth was void and empty, and darkness was upon the face of the deep; and the Spirit of God moved over the waters" (Ge 1:1–2). Although the concept of the Three Persons of the Trinity was unknown to the Jews, this passage of Holy Scripture reveals to us that they had an idea of the Spirit of God. Also in the Old Testament, we sometimes read that the Spirit of God comes upon someone, as it did upon Azarias, the son of Oded, and Zacharias, the son of Joiada, enabling them to prophesy (II Ch 15:1; II Ch 24:20). Actually, there are many references to the Spirit of God in the Old Testament. We cite only one more.

In the book of Zechariah, we learn how the Spirit of God is a mighty force in the lives of His people, enabling them to do His will. Upon the return from Babylon, the people are discouraged about rebuilding the temple, and Zechariah has a vision when an angel wakens him, asking him what he sees. To which the prophet replies that he sees a golden candlestick with a lamp upon the top of it, bearing seven lights that have seven funnels for them and two olive trees, one on either side of the candlestick (4:1–3). His curiosity piqued, Zechariah inquires of the angel, "What are these things, my lord? (4:40). The angel explains:

"This is the word of the Lord to Zorobabel, saying: 'Not with an army, nor by might, but by my Spirit,' says the Lord of Hosts. 'Who are you, O great mountain, before Zorobabel? You shall become a plain, and he shall bring out the chief stone, and shall give equal grace to the grace thereof.'"

We need to explain that Zorobabel, also spelled Zerubbabel, a descendant of King David, was appointed governor of the people of God when King Cyrus in 548 BC, promulgated an edit permitting them to return to Palestine and their homeland after a long exile. There was much discouragement about rebuilding the temple, and very little was accomplished for quite a while, although work began about 529 BC.

The prophecy given by the angel to Zechariah signifies that Zorobabel will rebuild the temple with the Spirit of God and not with might or armies. The angel completes the prophecy by saying: "The hands of Zorobabel have laid the foundations of this house, and his hands shall finish it" (4:0).

The New Testament has many, many references to the Holy Spirit. The Scripture tells us that Mary conceived by the power of the Holy Spirit. When Jesus was baptized in the River Jordan, the Holy Spirit descended upon him in the form of a dove. However, it was not until Jesus rose from the dead and ascended into heaven, that the Holy Spirit was poured out like a mighty river upon the nascent Church. In the Old Testament, the Spirit of God comes over people, but in the New Testament He indwells them.

The book of Acts might be described as the Gospel of the Holy Spirit, because it tells of His descent at Pentecost and of the wonderful things He did in the life of the early Church. In fact, in earlier days, this book was known as "The Gospel of the Holy Ghost" and also as "The Gospel of the Resurrection."

As one who knows Him intimately, St. Paul writes gloriously of the Holy Spirit in his epistles. Very much aware of the power of the Holy Spirit, Paul writes: "For our gospel has not been unto you in word only, but in power also, and in the Holy Ghost, and in much fullness, as you know what manner of men we have been among you for your sakes" (I Tm 1:5). And in the second letter to Timothy, he says: "For God hath not given us the spirit of fear, but of power, and of love, and of sobriety" (1:7).

In describing God's ministers, the writer of the book of Hebrews says that He makes them a flame of fire (1:7). This is certainly true of the Apostle Paul who was a veritable flame of fire that burned brightly throughout the ancient world and continues to blaze in his epistles down through the ages. As he says: "And my speech and my preaching was not in the persuasive words of human wisdom, but in showing of the Spirit and power" (I Co 2: 4). Explaining his preaching, Paul writes: "By the virtue of signs and wonders, in the power of the Holy Ghost, so that from Jerusalem round about as far as unto Illyricum, I have replenished the gospel of Christ" (Ro 16: 19). Paul's faith and ours are based on the power of the Holy Spirit.

According to Paul, we cannot even say "Jesus is Lord" without the Holy Spirit. "Wherefore I give you to understand, that no man, speaking by the Spirit of God, says Anathema to Jesus. And no man can say the Lord Jesus, but by the Holy Ghost" (I Co 12:3). The Spirit leads us in prayer, because we do not know what we should pray for (Ro 8:26). He searches the deep things of God and reveals them to us (I Co 2:10). "Now we have received not the spirit of this world, but the Spirit that is of God; that we may know the things that are given us from God (I Co 2:12).

One of the main points of Paul's teaching is that the Church is the temple of the Holy Spirit. To the Corinthians he writes: "Know you not, that you are the temple of God, and that the Spirit of God dwells in you?" (I Co 3:16). This point he reiterates: "Do you not know that your members are the temple of the Holy Ghost, who is in you, whom you have from God, and you are not your own?" (I Co 6:19). We belong to Him, because of His indwelling. Paul makes it very clear that we must be careful not to grieve the Holy Spirit (Ep 4:30) and "extinguish the Spirit," driving Him from our souls, by being insensitive and unresponsive to his inspirations and by sin (I Th 5:19).

Paul emphasizes that if the Spirit does not dwell in us, we do not belong to Christ (Ro 7:9). If we are His, the Spirit dwells within us, giving testimony that we are the sons and daughters of God (Ro 8:16). If we are joined to the Lord we are one spirit in Him (I Co 6: 17). We who are in Christ, in the Church, are being built into a "habitation of God in the Spirit" (Ep 2:22). Therefore we must be careful to keep "the unity of the Spirit in the bond of peace" (Ep 4:3).

Manifestation of the indwelling Spirit is given to everyone (I Co 12: 7). Paul elaborates on this as he describes how the various charisms are given in the Church.

> To one indeed, by the Spirit, is given the word of wisdom; and to another, the word of knowledge, according to the same Spirit; to another, faith in the same Spirit; to another; the grace of healing in one Spirit; to another, the working of miracles; to another, prophecy; to another, the discerning of spirits; to another; diverse kinds of tongues; to another, interpretation of speeches. But all these things one and the same Spirit works, dividing to every one according as He wills. For as the body is one, and hath many members, and all the members of the body, whereas they are many, yet are one body, so also is Christ.

> For in one Spirit were we all baptized into one body, whether Jews or Gentiles, whether bond or free; and in one Spirit, we have all been made to drink. (I Co 12: 8–13)

As we behold His glory, the Spirit of the Lord is transforming us into the image of Christ (II Co 3:18). The fruit of the Spirit in us is love, joy, peace, patience, kindness, graciousness, forbearance, mildness, faith, modesty, self-restraint, moderation, and chastity (Ga 5:18–23). As the creed confesses, He is the Lord and Giver of Life, and He gives life and peace to our minds, souls, and bodies. The kingdom of God is justice, and peace, and joy in the Holy Spirit (Ro 14:17). And because He dwells in us, He that raised Jesus from the dead will give life to us (Ro 8:11). He is our pledge of eternal life.

A second-century Bishop of Lyons, St. Irenaeus, who received the apostolic teaching from St. Polycarp (69–155) makes a trenchant comment about the Holy Spirit in *Adversus Haereses*, summing up his beliefs about Him. "But we now receive a certain portion of His Spirit, tending towards perfection, and preparing us for incorruption, being little by little accustomed to receive and bear God" (8.1). The Holy Spirit perfects us, guides us into receiving the Trinity into our souls and gradually makes it possible for us to bear more and more of Him until we come to incorruption in the Kingdom of Heaven.

Discoursing in his catechetical lectures, St. Cyril, Bishop of Jerusalem and Doctor of the Church (ca 315–386) remarked centuries ago "there is no satiety in concerning the Holy Spirit" (17). The lectures that he gave to converts to the Catholic Church in Jerusalem over sixteen hundred years ago are as fresh and poignant as if they had been written yesterday. He has much to say about the Holy Spirit whom he describes in this way:

> Now the Holy Spirit is a Power most mighty, a Being divine and unsearchable, for He is living and intelligent, a sanctifying principle of all things made by God through Christ. He it is who illuminates the souls of the just; He was in the Prophets, He was also in the Apostles." (16.3)

Cyril describes the coming of the Spirit as gentle. "The perception of Him is fragrant; His burden most light. Beams of light and knowledge gleam forth before His coming" (16.16). He enlightens the souls of men so that they can see things that are beyond the sight of others.

It is the Holy Spirit, Cyril reminds us, that sustains the martyrs, for He is the Comforter who encourages and comforts us. He gives gifts to all who are open to Him. "And as the light, with one touch of its radiance sheds brightness on all things, so also the Holy Spirit enlightens those who have eyes, for if any, from blindness, is not vouchsafed His grace, let him not blame the Spirit, but his own unbelief." According to Saint Cyril, it is our own fault, if we do not receive the gifts and the fruits of the Holy Spirit in great abundance. If we do not grieve the Holy Spirit by committing sin, Cyril assures us that He will be our guardian our entire lives, giving to us enormous graces.

A contemporary of St. Cyril of Jerusalem, St. Basil the Great, Bishop of Caesarea and a Doctor of the Church (329–379), wrote a magnificent treatise on the Holy Spirit, at the beginning of which, he explains the indwelling of the Spirit in the souls of the just.

> Now the Spirit is not brought into intimate association with the soul by local approximation. How indeed could there be a corporeal approach to the incorporeal? This association results from the withdrawal of the passions which, coming afterwards gradually on the soul from its friendship to the flesh, have alienated it from its close relationship with God. Only then after a man is purified from the shame whose stain he took through his wickedness, and has come back again to his natural beauty, and as it were cleaning the Royal Image and restoring its ancient form, only thus is it possible for him to draw near to the Paraclete. And He, like the sun, will, by the aid of your purified eye, show you in Himself the image of the invisible, and in the blessed spectacle of the image, you shall behold the unspeakable beauty of the archetype. Through His aid, hearts are lifted up, the weak are held by the hand, and they who are advancing are brought to perfection. Shining upon those that are cleansed from every spot, He makes them spiritual by fellowship with Himself. Just as when a sunbeam falls on bright and transparent bodies, they themselves become brilliant too, and shed forth a fresh brightness from themselves, so souls, wherein the Spirit dwells, illuminated by the Spirit, themselves become spiritual, and send forth their grace to others. (23)

Every gift, says St. Basil, comes to earth by way of the Holy Spirit (24:55). All praise should take place in Him, for the Lord has given us the power of beholding and contemplating Him. "It follows that the Spirit is verily the place of the saints and the saint is the proper place for the Spirit, offering himself as he does for the indwelling of God, and called God's Temple" (27:62). According to St. Basil, we receive from the Holy Spirit "according to the measure of our purification from evil, as we receive one a larger and another smaller share of the aid of the Spirit, that we may offer "the sacrifice of praise to God" (27:63). By the illumination the Holy Spirit gives, we are able to behold the brightness of the glory of God (27:64).

A contemporary of both St. Cyril of Jerusalem and St. Basil the Great, St. Ambrose, Bishop of Milan and Doctor of the Church (340–397) also wrote a splendid treatise on the Holy Spirit. Surely the writings of these three great Doctors of the Church on the Holy Spirit are some of the Spirit's most treasured gifts to the Church.

To St. Ambrose, the Holy Spirit is unction that he calls "ointment." "Now many have thought that the Holy Spirit is the ointment of Christ, and well it is said ointment, because He is called the oil of gladness, the joining together of many graces, giving a sweet fragrance" (100). He is the oil of gladness who makes us rejoice and sustains the martyrs, and "destroys the odor of sorrowful death" (100).

When the Holy Spirit shines His radiance into our souls, we behold the beauty of divine truth. Some people behold more of the truth than others, for each receives according to what the Lord gives (92). However, no one receives the Spirit wholly, because only Christ is capable of receiving Him completely. St. Ambrose makes the same observation, as does St. Basil, that the Spirit is not intimately united to the soul by "local approximation." "When we read that God is within or without, we certainly do not either enclose God within anybody or separate Him from anybody, but weighing these things in a deep and ineffable estimation, we comprehend the hiddenness of the divine nature" (119).

We also can never separate the Spirit from the Father or from the Son. The Persons of the Trinity are inseparable. He writes:

> The Holy Spirit, therefore, is not to be supposed to come separately. But He comes not from place to place, but from the disposition of the order to the safety of redemption, from the grace of giving life to that of sanctification, to translate us from earth to heaven, from wretchedness to glory, from slavery to a kingdom (122).

When the Spirit comes to us, the presence of the Father and the Son are in Him (123). "The Son and the Spirit are One, the Name of the Trinity is one, and the Presence one and indivisible" (159).

To Ambrose, the Holy Spirit is the Fount of Eternal Life, a great ever-flowing river that never fails, making glad the city of God (179). To know Him is life (180).

> For neither is that city, the heavenly Jerusalem, watered by the channel of any earthly river, but that Holy Spirit, proceeding from the Fount of Life, by a short draught of Whom we are satiated, seems to flow more abundantly

among those celestial Thrones, Dominions and Powers, Angels and Archangels, rushing in the full course of the seven virtues of the Spirit. For if a river rising above its banks overflows, how much more does the Spirit, rising above every creature, when He touches the, as it were, low-lying fields of our minds, make glad that heavenly nature of the creatures with the larger fertility of His sanctification. (178)

Anyone wishing to know more of what the Fathers of the Church have to say about the Holy Spirit should read the homilies of St. John Chrysostom (ca 347–407), Bishop of Constantinople and Doctor of the Church, on the book of Acts. Having the reputation of being a very great preacher, he had the ability to express himself in polished phrases. We present one example of the kinds of things he said; it is taken from homily IV. "Observe, how when one is continuing in prayer, when one is in charity, then it is that the Spirit draws near, for wherever the Holy Spirit is present, He makes men of gold out of men of clay."

Other Fathers of the Church one might read to learn more about the Holy Spirit are St. Cyprian of Carthage (martyred 258), St. Augustine of Hippo (354–386), and St. Gregory of Nyssa (d ca 386), among others. Time and space prevent us from writing more about the Holy Spirit in the early Church, and we now turn to *Divinum Illud Munu,* the encyclical of Leo XIII (1810–1903) on the Holy Spirit. Since the Holy Spirit is the one who inspires the Church, one is not surprised to see the great continuity in the teaching that continues down through the ages. To each writer is revealed something about the Holy Spirit that has not been previously known. Each author expresses some truths about the Holy Spirit that contribute to our knowledge. Leo XIII builds on what St. Augustine wrote, especially in his *De Trinitate*, and also on the writings of St. John Chrysostom, St. Cyril, and other of the Church Fathers. Regarding the indwelling of the Holy Spirit and the other Persons of the Trinity in the souls of the just, Leo XIII writes:

> Moreover, God by grace resides in the just soul as in a temple, in a most intimate and peculiar manner. From this proceeds that union of affection by which the soul adheres most closely to God, more so than the friend is united to his most loving and beloved friend, and enjoys God in all fullness and sweetness. Now this wonderful union, which is properly called "indwelling," differing only in degree or state from that with which God beatifies the saints in heaven, although it is most certainly produced by the presence of the whole Blessed Trinity—"We will come to Him and make our abode with Him," (John xiv. 23)—nevertheless is attributed in a peculiar manner to the Holy Spirit. For, whilst traces of divine power and wisdom appear even in the

wicked man, charity, which, as it were, is the special mark of the Holy Ghost, is shared in only by the just. In harmony with this, the same Spirit is called Holy, for He, the first and supreme Love, moves souls and leads them to sanctity, which ultimately consists in the love of God. (9)

Because of the indwelling of the Holy Spirit, we should "direct towards Him the highest homage of our love and devotion (10). We should strive every day to know Him better and to love Him more.

Leo points out that remission of our sins comes from the Holy Spirit. However it is not enough to flee from sin. "Every Christian ought to shine with the splendor of virtue so as to be pleasing to so great and so beneficent a guest; and first of all with chastity and holiness, for chaste and holy things befit the temple" (10). One of the most striking statements in the encyclical is "if Christ is the Head of the Church, the Holy Spirit is its soul."

One of the greatest theologians of the 20th century, Yves Congar, wrote a monumental work in three volumes titled *I Believe in the Holy Spirit*. In volume one, *The Holy Spirit in the "Economy": Revelation and Experience of the Spirit,* he begins with the Spirit of God, the Breath of Yahweh in the Old Testament and traces His activity through the writings of the prophets, citing Ezechiel (36:35–27, 37:3–5, and 39:39) in which God promises to send forth his Spirit into the hearts of His people.

And I will pour upon you clean water, and you shall be cleansed from all your filthiness, and I will cleanse you from all your idols. And I will give you a new heart, and put a new spirit within you, and I will take away the stony heart out of your flesh, and will give you a heart of flesh. And I will put my spirit in the midst of you, and I will cause you to walk in my commandments, and to keep my judgments, and do them.

After tracing the Spirit of God through the wisdom literature, Congar concludes the chapter on the Old Testament, saying, "In the Jewish Bible, the Breath-Spirit of God is the action of God" (12). Though His Spirit, God gives life and animates nature.

In discussing the work of the Spirit in the New Testament, Congar declares that Pentecost was for the Church what Jesus' baptism in the Jordan was for Christ—"the gift and the power of the Spirit, dedication to the ministry, mission and bearing witness" (19). He gives a summary of St. Paul's teaching on the Holy Spirit. On commenting of the book of Acts, Congar notes that Pentecost is a paschal feast and that there are no feasts of the Persons of the Trinity (45).

In the writings of the saints, in the liturgy, and in various documents, including those of Vatican II, Congar shows the development of the teaching about the Holy Spirit down through the centuries.

Volume II of Congar's work, *The Lord and Giver of Life*, speaks of the way in which the Spirit animates the Church and makes it one. Interestingly, Congar observes that the role of authority has been overemphasized in the Church. "In the modern era, excessive emphasis has been given in the Catholic Church to the role of authority, and there has been a juridical tendency to reduce order to an observance of imposed rules, and unity to uniformity" (16). Because of the system of supervision which is designed to maintain orthodoxy, many individuals have been marginalized and even silenced.

Congar sees the Holy Spirit, the principle of holiness in the Church, as being the principle of her catholicity and of keeping her apostolic. To him: "The Church then is a sign of the presence of God" (58).

In discussing life in the Spirit and our prayer life, Congar defines prayer by quoting Charles Foucauld's definition—"praying is thinking of God while loving Him" (115). This is surely a beautiful definition of prayer. He concludes: The Holy Spirit "is our union with God and for that reason he is our prayer" (117).

While Congar writes about the charismatic renewal in the Church and the charisms, one feels that his approach is academic and lacks the experiential dimension that the Fathers of the Church knew and expressed in their writings.

In Volume III, *The River of the Water of Life Flows in the East and the West*, Congar attempts to reconcile the different view concerning the procession of the Holy Spirit that is held in the Eastern Orthodox Church with that of Rome.

While Congar's three volumes are a massive work of scholarship, they do not have the unction that we found in the writings of the great Fathers of the early Church that we discussed previously. To find that unction in the present day writing on the Holy Spirit we turn to *Dominum et Vivificantum*, an encyclical of John Paul II. If John Paul had not written anything besides *Dominum et Vivificantum*, he would go down in history as John Paul the Great. Not only does this encyclical contain brilliant original theological thinking, but it is filled with the unction of the Holy Spirit, because it is written by a holy man who personally knows the Holy Spirit intimately. Anyone who wishes to know the Holy Spirit, and not just know facts about Him, should read this magnificent work.

Basically, John Paul II sees the Holy Spirit as continuing the presence and the work of the Redeemer on earth (7). The Holy Spirit is personal love and in Him, the Trinity becomes "totally gift" (10). It was necessary for Jesus to leave this world to make it possible for the Holy Spirit to come to us, beginning what John

Paul terms "the new salvific self-giving of God in the Holy Spirit" (11). The Risen Christ brings the Holy Spirit, and this could not have happened, if it had not been for the Crucifixion and Resurrection (24). Pentecost is perpetuated in the Church down through the centuries by the bishops who have received the Spirit by the laying on of hands and give the Spirit to others in the sacraments of holy orders and confirmation (25).

The Holy Spirit acted in a special way in Christ's redemptive suffering, in order to transform it into redemptive love (40). The Holy Spirit as Love and Gift comes down, in a certain sense, into the very heart of the sacrifice which is offered on the Cross. Referring here to the biblical tradition, we can say: He consumes this sacrifice with the fire of love which unites the Son with the Father in the Trinitarian communion. And since the sacrifice of the Cross is an act proper to Christ, also in this sacrifice He "receives" the Holy Spirit (41).

Distributing His fruits, the Holy Spirit applies the work of redemption to the souls of the people (46). According to John Paul II, the conception and birth of Jesus are the greatest work of the Holy Spirit in the history of creation (50). He sees the incarnation as having a cosmic dimension, because Jesus took the whole of humanity and the entire physical world into unity with God (50).

Man receives the fullness of freedom when God, in the Holy Spirit, opens Himself to man. This thought makes it possible for John Paul to define faith as the opening of the human heart to God's self-communication in the Spirit. Mary's faith shows forth the fullness of freedom, because of her complete self-giving (51).

God, as absolute Spirit, is present in this world, especially in relation to man's being, mind, conscience and heart (54). Because human life is permeated by the divine life, it "acquires a divine, supernatural dimension" (52). Through the power of the Spirit, Christ is present in the Church, making it His own body (61). It is the Spirit who gives life (64).

> The breath of the divine life, the Holy Spirit, in its simplest and most common manner, expresses itself and makes itself felt in prayer. It is a beautiful and salutary thought that, wherever people are praying in the world, there the Holy Spirit is, the living breath of prayer. (65)

The Holy Spirit breathes prayer into the abyss in the heart of man that only He can fill (65). With the help of the Holy Spirit, our prayer becomes a participation in the divine life.

John Paul describes the Holy Spirit as the Spirit of Peace.

Peace too is the fruit of love: that interior peace, which weary man seeks in his inmost being; that peace besought by humanity, the human family, peoples, nations, continents, anxiously hoping to obtain it in the prospect of the transition from the second to the third Christian Millennium. Since the way of peace passes in the last analysis through love and seeks to create the civilization of love, the Church fixes her eyes on him who is the love of the Father and the Son, and in spite of increasing dangers she does not cease to trust, she does not cease to invoke and to serve the peace of man on earth. Her trust is based on him who, being the Spirit-love, is also the Spirit of peace and does not cease to be present in our human world, on the horizon of minds and hearts, in order to "fill the universe" with love and peace. (67)

Let us seek peace where it is to be found—in the Holy Spirit in the heart of the Trinity. Let us draw near to Him in prayer and wait for His inspirations to draw us closer to Jesus and the Heavenly Father. He is nearer than breathing, as St. Paul says, and closer than hands and feet. He does not hide Himself from us. Rather, it is we ourselves who prevent us, by our coldness of heart and failure to respond to His inspirations, from entering into the fullness He wishes to bestow upon us. We must learn to be responsive to the stirrings of the Holy Spirit within us and as the Holy Scripture says: "Today if you shall hear His voice, harden not your hearts" (Heb 4:7–8).

"Sweet Holy Spirit, we will listen for your inspirations and faithfully try to follow them. We will keep our hearts tender toward You, so that you may lead and guide us to Jesus who is the way to the Father. Holy Trinity, live in us that we may live in You and never be separated from You in time or eternity. Fill us with Your love and peace that we may become true children of God and peacemakers in our troubled world. Help us to know You better so that we may serve You more effectively and respond to Your every inspiration. In Jesus name, we pray in union with the Holy Spirit to the glory of God the Father. Amen."

7

Peace at Home

When we consider the Holy Family we realize that they are a model for family life, although they do not resemble us in many ways. They were an exceptional family because the mother was a virgin throughout her married life, the son was the Lord of the mother, and the father was not a real father. Nevertheless, they teach us a great deal about how to have peace at home. We especially learn from the Blessed Mother from the way she relates to God, the angel Gabriel, and the people of her life. She is truly our Queen of Peace.

St. Luke relates that the angel Gabriel was sent to Nazareth to visit Mary, a virgin engaged to marry Joseph. The angel greeted her saying: "Hail, full of grace, the Lord is with you: blessed are you among women" (1:28). Mary listened to the angel and was attentive to the messenger of the Lord and the message He had to bring her. She had time to listen, understand what he was saying, and be attentive to the will of God. Consequently, the life of the Holy Family was built on the Word of God.

How many young people today would have time to listen to an angel and pay attention to what he says? We need to be attentive to the will of God and open our hearts to hear His voice. We need to form our family life upon the Word of God, and what it has to say to us.

Not only was Mary careful to listen to the angel and discern the will of God, she was attentive to people. She was alert to the problem of the couple being married at Cana, and told Jesus that they had run out of wine. Just as Mary cared about what was going on in the lives of people around her, we need to be attentive to what is happening in the lives of people we know and perceive their needs. We must observe people and notice the signals they are giving us, because people do give signals when something is wrong in their lives. We need to discover, if they are lacking wine at their feast. We need to care.

The first thing we need to do, then, to have peace at home is to pay attention to God and the people around us. Consider this story of a ten year old boy who wants to know how much money his father makes for an hour's work. Because the dad is busy watching a NFL football game on television, he expresses annoyance and says: "Leave me alone. Can't you see I am watching the game?"

A little while later, the child returns and once again asks: "How much money do you make an hour, Daddy?"

"Don't bother me now. I'll talk to you at half time."

When the boy returns at half time, he again asks: "Daddy, how much money *do* you make an hour." To get rid of the child, the father brushes him off saying, "Thirty dollars. Now go play and let me watch the game."

When bedtime comes, the father proceeds to tuck the child into his bed, asking him: "Why do you want to know how much money I make an hour?"

"Because I want to borrow ten dollars from you."

The father gives the child the ten dollars. Immediately, the child opens his piggy bank and pulls out twenty dollars and hands it to his father, together with the ten that he borrowed. When the father asks what the money is for the child replies: "I want to buy an hour of your time."

We simply do not have time for the people who mean the most to us. We just do not listen to what they have to say. Husbands do not listen to their wives; parents do not listen to their children. We need to make time to listen and open our ears, when people want to talk. Most importantly we need to listen with our hearts. We will enjoy life more if we learn to listen.

Why do we not listen? Because we are selfish and have our plans and our agendas. Sometimes, we simply have to give up our plans and put those we love ahead of what we intended to do. Our relationships with family and friends must take priority over the things we are addicted to, such as television, shopping, talking on the phone, or what have you. All too often, our activities become more important than being attentive and receptive to the needs of others.

When we learn the beauty of paying attention to others, we relax, feel content, and at peace. We really do not need things to make us happy. If we do not depend on things to satisfy us, we are able to love people more. We must put loving in first place in our lives. We must free ourselves so that we can love people, for loving is the most important thing in the life of a believer in Jesus Christ.

Some people say that living in their house is like residing in hell, or purgatory at best. How can anyone survive, if he has to fight in the world to earn a living and then come home to turmoil? The most important thing is to enjoy family and friends and have peace at home. In order to have peace at home, the first thing we must do is be attentive to the needs of others. Loving fights stress.

When little children cry or whine, we try to take care of their needs. What they are telling us is that they need us and need our love. As we pay attention to them, their yelling stops. Some adults are like children who never grow up. They are always whining and complaining to make themselves feel important. If we tell them to relax and be happy, they often respond the way children do and stop fussing. We need to understand the needs of others and help to meet than, so that we can enjoy peace at home.

We need to consider who needs our attention. There are many people who are knocking on our doors, seeking to be heard. We need to make a priority list of the people who need us, and then we should pay attention to them. When they get the attention they need, they will be happy and we will be free to enjoy peace.

The second thing we must do to have peace at home is to cultivate understanding. The Blessed Mother gives us an excellent example of this. In St. Luke's gospel, we read that when the shepherds visited the new-born Christ Child, and told people how the angels had visited them in the fields, telling them of the birth of the Savior, "Mary kept all these words, pondering them in her heart (Luke 2: 19). Later, when Mary and Joseph went to the temple to present Jesus to the Lord, and to offer the sacrifice of a pair of turtledoves or two young pigeons, a man named Simeon was there, and he spoke under the inspiration of the Holy Spirit. He took the child Jesus in his arms and proclaimed that his eyes were beholding the salvation of God, saying:

> "Now dismiss your servant, O Lord, according to your word in peace, because my eyes have seen your salvation, which you have prepared before the face of all peoples—a light to the revelation of the Gentiles, and the glory of your people Israel." (Lk 2:27–32)

Luke records that both Mary and Joseph wondered about the things Simeon said (2:33).

Still later when Jesus was twelve years old, he got separated from Mary and Joseph, and stayed behind in the Temple at Jerusalem, when the family was returning to Nazareth. When they discovered that Jesus was missing, they returned to Jerusalem and found Him in the Temple. The Holy Scripture tells us:

> And it came to pass, that, after three days, they found Him in the temple, sitting in the midst of the doctors, hearing them, and asking them questions. And all that heard Him were astonished at His wisdom and His answers, and seeing Him, they wondered. And His mother said to Him: "Son, why have

you done so to us? Behold your father and I have sought You sorrowing." And He said to them: "How is it that you sought Me? Did you not know, that I must be about My Father's business?" And they understood not the word that He spoke unto them. (Lk 2:46–50).

Here we see how Mary and Jesus resolved their problem with effective dialogue and that bound them closer together as a family. Because she did not understand, Mary had many things to ponder in her heart. We can learn understanding from her. We can never understand all that is taking place in the hearts of those around us. Therefore, we must let them be themselves and be compassionate toward them, for there will always be things we cannot understand.

Some people who have lived together for twenty years or longer are still fighting. Surely after all that time, they should have learned to live together in peace. Perhaps he can never learn to replace the cap on the toothpaste in the mornings and she is a born nagger. Some things we just have to accept for the sake of peace.

It is difficult to figure people out. St. Paul said he had trouble figuring himself out. "For that which I work, I understand not. For I do not that good which I will; but the evil which I hate, that I do" (Ro 7:15). Just like St. Paul, we have good intentions, but we do not follow through with them. There is weakness in our lives. Other people are just like we are and have weakness in their lives as well. We might have the best intentions in the world, but people cannot read our minds, and see what we are hoping to do. We need to express our thoughts and feelings clearly, so that those we live with will understand and know what to expect of us. If we want people to remember something, such as our birthday, we should drop little hints, so that they will not absentmindedly overlook something that is important to us.

A typical conversation between a man and his wife might run something like this:

Joe: "What's going on?" He notices she is rather cold toward him.

Molly: "Nothing." She turns her back on him and walks a few feet away.

Joe: "What is the trouble?" He looks puzzled.

Molly: "Nothing at all. I am all right." She sounds offended.

Joe: "What is wrong?"

Molly: "You *know* what is wrong!" She answers with great annoyance.

Poor Joe has no idea what is bothering his wife.

We should tell people how we feel and let them know what our needs are. We also need to confess our fears and realize that it is all right to have fears. When we confess them and acknowledge them, we can then return to being courageous again. We need to be able to express what is in our hearts. We have to make ourselves understood. To be sure that we are understood, we have to ask, "Am I making myself clear?"

It is important that we do not worry about what people will think, but we should concern ourselves with what we should tell them. If we are happy or sad, we should explain why we are so.

A third way of peace that we can learn from the Blessed Mother can be found in the *Magnificat*. "And Mary said: My soul does magnify the Lord. And my spirit has rejoiced in God my Savior" (Lk 3:46–47). Mary celebrates her joy in the Lord. Christian life is one of celebration. We celebrate Jesus present in the Eucharist and in the community of believers. Celebration is what Christianity is all about.

With Mary we need to rejoice in the Lord. There is much pain in life, but we need to forget the pain and celebrate and rejoice in God. God is life-giving. So we are getting on in life, and the doctor tells us that we only have six months more to live. How do we react to this news? We can consider that we have had many, many good years. We do not have to believe the doctor. We believe that God wants to give us life in this world or the next. Let us then celebrate the joy of knowing the Lord and Giver of Life! Let us then rejoice in the good things God has given us—family, friends, and our home. Let us then enjoy all the gifts the Lord has given us. Some people work all their lives and never take time to enjoy the blessings of God. Everyday we should celebrate the goodness of the Lord.

In this country, we have many material things, but the beauty of life is not based on things we can acquire. It is based on love and the relationships we have with God and other people. When we celebrate, the Holy Spirit turns everything into a blessing. Everything depends on our attitude—everything should be festive for the believer.

We learn from Mary to face things as they come and be practical and concrete in our approach to them. When she gave birth to Jesus in a stable, she took a manger, a feeding trough for the animals, and made it into a cradle. We need to face life in the same way, taking it as it comes. We solve our problems with dialogue, and after we resolve them, we do something concrete to bind us closer together. In this way, we have peace in the home.

We need tenderness in our relationships with our family and friends. Consider the tenderness with which Mary received the body of Jesus, when He came down off the cross. All too often, we take our family and friends for granted, and treat the ones that are closest to us the worst. If people spoke to their friends the way they speak to family members, they would have no friends. Tenderness is the element that makes the difference in a relationship. We need to love people in a visible, affectionate way, caring for their feelings and their needs. We need honey not vinegar in dealing with people. Life is nicer when it is sweeter.

We learn about relationships when we consider that as Jesus was dying on the cross, he gave his mother to St. John.

> When Jesus therefore had seen His mother and the disciple standing whom He loved, He said to His mother: "Woman, behold your son." After that, He said to the disciple: "Behold your mother." And from that hour, the disciple took her to his own. (Jn 19:26–27)

At this time, a new relationship was created. Mary was a gift to John and John to Mary. Here we recall that Jesus said: "For whosoever shall do the will of My Father that is in heaven, He is my brother, and sister, and mother" (Mt 12:50). Relationships that are founded on the will of God are stronger than natural human relationships. As Mary was a gift to John and John to Mary we, too, are gifts to other people. We are God's gift to those who accept us as such, when we accept those we love as God's gift to us. When we treat each other as gifts of God, life is more beautiful and more blessed. When we realize that the friend we love is a gift of God, we treat him/her with greater care and affection. As we appreciate the family and friends God gives us, we understand the beauty of our natural family and of our extended family in Christ.

"Heavenly Father, we ask you to make us sensitive to other people and attentive to their needs. May we try to understand and accept them as they are, treating them with love and tenderness, so that we may grow closer to each other and to You. May we be open with those we love and tell them the needs that we experience, and may we, with listening hearts, respond to them. May we realize that those we love are Your gifts to us to teach how to love and to be loved in return. We thank you that you have given us the Blessed Mother as an example of how we are to live in peace in our homes. Amen."

"Our Lady, Queen of Peace, pray for us!"

8

Peace of Mind

Some of us have no peace of mind, because we are too concerned about what people think of us, are troubled with feelings of guilt, or are perfectionists that want to control everything.

Many of us have a poor self-image that keeps us constantly in turmoil. Perhaps we feel inferior, because we are not as well educated as we might have wished. Others feel rejected, because of something in their makeup. Perhaps their parents rejected them as children, and they have not learned to put these feelings of rejection aside. Maybe we feel clumsy and gauche, when we are at a social gathering, because we never learned the proper social graces. Perhaps we feel inferior, because we are women employed by a boss who denigrates women.

To have peace of mind we must get rid of all feelings of rejection and unworthiness. How can we do this? We must consider that we are children of the Most High God who created us. If He made us and has adopted us as His children, there must be good in us. God does not make junk, and He loves His children. We must become deeply aware of His love for us, just like the little children who sing in Bible School, "Jesus loves me, this I know, for the Bible tells me so." The Bible indeed does tell us that God loves us. "Yes, I have loved you with everlasting love" (Jr 31:3).

When we have feelings of inferiority, let us look in the mirror and see ourselves with all our flaws and failings and say: "God loves ME—just the way I am! He has chosen me to be His temple, for the Persons of the Trinity came to dwell in me, when I was baptized." God comes into the most intimate corners of our hearts to fill us with His love, so that we will live with Him forever in His mercy, pardon, joy, strength, and power. We need not fear anyone or anything, because the Spirit of God is within us, and we can do all things in Christ who gives us the strength. This was the secret of St. Paul's ability to survive multiple shipwrecks, persecutions, beatings, and finally decapitation, as he says: "I can do all things in Him who strengthens me" (Ph 4:13).

Let us steep ourselves in the love of God, and all thoughts of inferiority will vanish, especially when we begin to realize that God has a beautiful plan for our lives to give us happiness and joy. Jesus tells us: "I am come that they may have life, and may have it more abundantly" (Jn 10:10). He tells us to ask in prayer that our "joy may be full" (Jn 16:24). Jesus wants us to be happy and fulfilled with a happiness that begins in this life and blossoms into glory and joy unspeakable in the next.

The devil will try to destroy us by saying we are worthless. The devil is a liar and the prince of liars. People will say we are not as good as others. We do not compare ourselves to anyone, because we are unique—unlike anyone else God ever created or ever will create. Because He made us, we know there is something special about each one of us. Let us open the Word of God, and learn of His fantastic plans for us to receive His grace. In His Word, we find all we need to be happy and joyful now, and to be glorified in the life of the world to come.

Some people never find happiness, joy, and peace of mind, because they are troubled constantly by feelings of guilt. No matter how often they wash their hands, they feel like they have dirt under their fingernails that they cannot wash away. No matter how often they go to confession, they still feel guilty of some sin in the past, or perhaps have a general sense of guilt. Why is this? Let us consider the human conscience. Pope Paul VI wrote the following about the conscience in *Gaudium et Spes*, an encyclical dated December 7, 1965:

> In the depths of his conscience, man detects a law which he does not impose upon himself, but which holds him to obedience. Always summoning him to love good and avoid evil, the voice of conscience when necessary speaks to his heart: do this, shun that. For man has in his heart a law written by God; to obey it is the very dignity of man; according to it he will be judged. Conscience is the most secret core and sanctuary of a man. There he is alone with God, Whose voice echoes in his depths. In a wonderful manner conscience reveals that law which is fulfilled by love of God and neighbor. In fidelity to conscience, Christians are joined with the rest of men in the search for truth, and for the genuine solution to the numerous problems which arise in the life of individuals from social relationships. Hence the more right conscience holds sway the more persons and groups turn aside from blind choice and strive to be guided by the objective norms of morality. Conscience frequently errs from invincible ignorance without losing its dignity. The same cannot be said for a man who cares but little for truth and goodness, or for a conscience which by degrees grows practically sightless as a result of habitual sin.

His Holiness goes on to state the need for people to have well-formed consciences, so that "the divine law is inscribed in the life of the earthly city." If our consciences are not well formed, we can have feelings of guilt that never go away, no matter how often we receive the Sacrament of Reconciliation. Continual guilt feelings do not spring from a Christian conscience, because when God pardons, He pardons completely and permanently. The Holy Scripture assures us: "As far as the East is from the West, so far has He removed our iniquities from us" (Ps 102:12). Micah tells us: "He will turn again, and have mercy on us: He will put away our iniquities, and He will cast all our sins into the bottom of the sea" (7:19).

How does one form one's conscience? The psalmist tells us: "Your word is a lamp to my feet and a light to my paths" (118:105). We must let the Word of God form our conscience, in conjunction with the teachings of the Church, and together they will help us to discern good and evil in our thoughts and actions.

Unfortunately, we all do not have well-formed consciences. According to the *Catechism of the Catholic Church*, "A well-formed conscience is upright and truthful. It formulates its judgments according to reason, in conformity with the true good willed by the wisdom of the Creator" (1798).

Our consciences can trouble us and make us feel guilty, often because we have been inculcated with certain values that have nothing to do with ethics and morality. Perhaps we were taught to do certain things by our parents, and because we do not do them, we feel guilty. Perhaps a man feels guilty and ill at ease, because his car is not clean. Many housewives feel guilty because their house is not as clean and tidy as their inculcated set of values dictate, or as neat as their mother-in-law feels it should be. Some are addicted to keeping the house so spotless that the family does not feel comfortable living in it. There are even those who quickly start tidying up the house, because of feelings of compulsion, as soon as someone drops in to visit. We need to realize that the Holy Spirit is not going through our homes looking for every speck of dust to reproach us. We need to get rid of these false feelings of guilt that keep us from having peace of mind. People who suffer guilt from not keeping their inculcated set of values may also be perfectionists. We are not talking about people who are trying to be perfect like the Heavenly Father is perfect by growing in faith, hope and love, but about people who try to control everything within their sphere of influence. Some people, for example, compel their children to go into careers they are not suited for. How many mothers have tried to make their sons into priests or doctors without regard to their welfare?

When we are driven into trying to control everyone and everything and are guilt ridden, because we are not living up to expectations, we have no peace. This is because we are looking for peace where it is not to be found, causing us to turn to positive thinking gurus, or transcendental meditation, or Silva mind control, or something similar. Happiness is not to be found in these things. Only in Christ Jesus can we find true happiness, for the only thing that matters to us as Christians is to have His Spirit dwelling in our souls.

Positive thinking and similar teachings will tell us that we are the best people and that we are OK. We who are in Christ are far more than they imagine. We are unique creations of God. There has never been anyone like us in the past and there never will be another like us in the future. Just as we are—sinners, weak, mixed up, confused—Jesus Christ loves us! What if we are little and do not count for much in the eyes of the world? St. Paul tells us:

> But God has chosen the foolish things of the world to confound the wise; and God has chosen the weak things of the world to confound the things which are mighty; and base things of the world, and things which are despised, has God chosen, yes, and things which are not, to bring to naught things that are—that no flesh should glory in His presence. (I Co 1:26–29)

We must always remember that God did not send His Son into the world to condemn it, but to save it (Jn 3:17). Jesus offers us a plan of salvation, not condemnation. Salvation begins in this life the moment we say to Jesus Christ: "I want to walk with you. I want to have my name written in the book of life. I want to be with you in heaven."

We do not save ourselves. We cannot. Our positive thinking as Christians comes from the Word of God. We see we have defects, but if we were no good, we could not draw near to Him. Yes, we are weak, but in our weakness, the power of God reigns with His wisdom and power dwelling in us. He pardons us, and we draw near to Him. Because of His great love, He draws us to Himself. Then wonder of wonders! His love lifts us up and makes us the people He wants us to be. We enter His presence and kneel in adoration. We listen for His voice in the depths of our spirits.

We do not listen to the low opinions some people might have of us. God says He loves us, and His Word is certain. We need to develop positive identities and be sure of ourselves. If someone insults us, let us give him/her the benefit of the doubt, until we are sure that we really are being mistreated. If we decide we are, then we shake it off, recalling our dignity as sons and daughters of the Most High God. We then realize that it does not matter what people think of us. We are temples of the Holy Spirit and sons and daughters of the King of Kings. We shrug our shoulders and say, "It really doesn't matter." What if I did buy my clothes as a discount store instead of a place of high fashion? I am filled with love learned at the feet of Jesus on the cross.

Let the grace of God flood our hearts! Only Jesus can heal us of our worry about what people think of us, rid us of our guilt, and free us from a false perfectionism. We are new people in Christ. Let us renounce everything that holds us back from growing in His love. What really matters is that we are children of the Most High God, and we have been given so much by Him. We are alive—our sight, hearing, speaking—are all gifts of God, freely given, for He has no obligation to give us any gift or even another minute of life. Let us thank Him for all His gifts, especially the gift of life eternal. Every day we live is an exclusive gift of God. Let us listen to His word and let Him guide us and lead us to Himself and heaven. God loves us, pardons us, and tells us not to worry saying, "My child, don't worry about anything. I am with you. Peace be unto you!"

We are not to worry about bad times, because Christianity is a faith for all times. We are to thank God for everything—the good and the bad. St. Paul tells us we are to be "Giving thanks always for all things, in the name of our Lord Jesus Christ, to God and the Father" (Ep 5:20). Nothing should take away the peace of mind of a true believer in Jesus Christ. Jesus is much greater than our worst enemy.

> But in all these things we overcome, because of Him that has loved us. For I am sure that neither death, nor life, nor angels, nor principalities, nor powers, nor things present, nor things to come, nor might, nor height, nor depth, nor any other creature, shall be able to separate us from the love of God, which is in Christ Jesus our Lord. (Ro 8:37)

"Dear Lord, We are confident of Your love. Help us to live in peace with our past, our consciences and those around us. We are not afraid, because You are with us, and You have loved us with an everlasting love (Jr: 31:3). With St. Paul we say, 'I can do all these things in Him who strengthens me' (Ph 4:13). Heal us of our poor self-images, and take away our false feelings of guilt, and teach us how to walk in your ways of perfection. We thank you that You have not given us a spirit of fear, but of power and of love and of sobriety (II Tm 1:7). May Your wisdom guide us in the paths of truth that lead to peace and to heaven. We thank You for giving us peace. Amen"

9

Peace of Body

Our bodies are also meant to share in the peace of Christ, and if they are sick or in pain, we can not be completely at peace. We have a beautiful word from God that tells us that Christ suffered that we might be healed. The Prophet Isaiah foretold the coming of the Messiah and said: "He was wounded for our iniquities, he was bruised for our sins: the chastisement of our peace was upon him, and by his bruises we are healed" (53:5). Some translations say "by his stripes we are healed," because such were the bruises that he suffered for our healing. The Romans made a whip out of the sinews of oxen and put sharp pieces of bone in various places in the sinews so that when the scourge struck, the flesh was torn off down to the bone, and marks like stripes appeared on the body.

That the Lord God heals people's bodies is well documented throughout the Old Testament. Very clearly, God told Moses that He is a healing God, saying:

> If you will hear the voice of the Lord your God, and do what is right before Him, and obey His commandments, and keep all His precepts, none of the evils that I laid upon Egypt, will I bring upon you, for I am the Lord your healer. (Ex 15:26)

The Scripture expands on this in a later chapter of Exodus, saying: "And you shall serve the Lord your God, that I may bless your bread and your waters, and may take away sickness from the midst of you" (23:25).

If the Lord granted healing to the ancient Hebrews, when they kept his commandments, He will do the same for us. We know that the Lord is the same today as He was in the time of Moses, because we read in Holy Scripture in the book of Malachi: "For I am the Lord, I change not" (3:6). Therefore, we know that if we keep His commandments and precepts, He will be our healer too. In the book of Deuteronomy, we learn more about the promise made to Moses. "The Lord will take away from you all sickness, and the grievous infirmities of

Egypt, which you know, He will not bring upon you, but upon your enemies" (7:15). The Lord also promises long life to those who keep His commandments.

> Keep His precepts and commandments, which I command you that it may be well with you and your children after you, and you may remain a long time upon the land, which the Lord your God will give you. (De 4:40)

God gave Moses a long life, and when he died at an advanced old age, he was still strong and his vision still good (De 34:7).

One of the most beautiful stories of the healing power of God in the entire Bible is the miracle of the prophet Elisha in restoring the son of the Sunamite woman. Elisha—his name means "God is salvation"—was a disciple of the prophet Elijah and also his attendant. The restoration of the child by Elisha recalls Elijah's healing and restoration of the son of the widow of Sarephta of the Sidonians (I K 17:19). Since Elisha was chosen by Elijah to be his successor, it is no wonder that Elisha adopted the techniques of his mentor in dealing with people. However, he was quite different from Elijah in many respects. Elijah is described by the author of Ecclesiasticus, as arising life a fire and with his words blazing like a torch (58:1). He was a man of the desert, "a hairy man with a girdle of leather about his loins" that lived in caves or in clefts of streams, and who reproached Israel for their infidelity to God and the evil of the corrupt times (II K 1: 8). When he was in a cave at Horeb, the Lord told him to anoint Elisha as a prophet and as his successor, causing him to set out immediately to find Elisha, who was busy plowing his fields. Throwing his mantle over the shoulders of Elisha, he invested him as a prophet and adopted him as his son.

Accepting the call to become a prophet, Elisha killed his yoke of oxen and cooked them using the wood of his plough for firewood, making a complete and abrupt end of his life as a farmer. After sharing the dinner of oxen with his companions and a quick farewell, he departed straightaway to follow the great prophet Elijah.

In contrast to Elijah, Elisha was not a man of the desert, but a civilized man who wore the customary dress of the Israelites and carried a walking stick. One day Elisha and Elijah were on their way to the Jordan, about eight years after the call of Elisha, and shortly before the death of Elijah. When they came to the river, Elijah folded up his mantle and struck the water of the Jordan with it, dividing the water so that the two of them were able to cross on dry land. After they crossed the river, Elijah said to Elisha: "Ask what you will have me to do for you, before I be taken away from you." Elisha responded: "I beseech you that in me may be your double Spirit" (II K 2:9). He wanted a double portion of the Spirit that made Elijah a great prophet, able to do mighty works for God.

"You have asked a hard thing," replied Elijah, "nevertheless, if you see me when I am taken from you, you shall have what you have asked, if you see me not, you shall not have it? (II K 2:10). Elisha watched carefully as the angels came and took his father in God away to heaven. As the mantle of Elijah fell to the ground at his departure, Elisha picked it up and struck the waters of the Jordan with it as he had seen Elijah do. When the waters parted, he was convinced, and so were many others, that he had in fact received a double portion of the Spirit. For sixty years, he continued doing the same wonderful things he had seen Elijah do as prophet of God. The story of his healing and restoring the son of the Sunamite woman shows us much about the dispositions we should have in order for God to heal us.

One day Elisha visited Sunam, a village about five miles south of Mount Tabor, where an affluent woman invited him to a meal, because she knew him to be a holy man of God. She then told her husband:

> "I perceive that this is a holy man of God, who often passes by us. Let us therefore make him a little chamber, and put a little bed in it for him, and a table, and a stool, and a candlestick, that when he comes to us, he may abide there." (II K 4:8–9)

Her husband agreed and they prepared the room, and Elisha moved into it.

One day when he was in his room, Elisha asked his servant Giezi to call the woman and tell her the following:

> "Behold you have diligently served us in all things, what will you have me to do for you? Do you have any business, and do you want me to speak to the king or to the general of the army?" (II K 4:13)

She had no need of anything, so she replied: "I dwell in the midst of my own people" (II K 4:13). When Giezi relayed this information to Elisha, the prophet asked: "What will she then that I do for her?" (II K 4:14) The servant thought about it and told Elisha: "Do not ask, for she has no son, and her husband is old." Nevertheless, Elisha directed Giezi to summon the woman to come to him. When she appeared at the door of his room, Elisha told her that she was going to have a baby. In unbelief, the barren woman replied: "Do not, I beseech you, my lord, you man of God, do not lie to your handmaid" (4:16).

Elisha spoke the truth. In due season, his prophecy came true, and the baby was born, and, in time, grew into a nice boy child. One day, he went out into the fields with his father to watch the men who were reaping the crops. After a time the boy complained of having a headache, crying to his father, "My head aches! My head aches!" (4: 18).

The father directed a servant to carry the boy to his mother, who cuddled the boy in her arms and held him until noon, when the little fellow tragically died. At once, without saying a word to her husband about the child's death, she took her little boy to Elisha's room and placed him on the prophet's bed and closed the door behind her.

Still not telling her husband what had happened, she asked him to provide her with a servant and an ass so that she could go find the man of God and fetch him, saying: "Send with me, I beseech you, one of your servants and an ass that I may run to the man of God." It was the custom for a servant to be in charge of the animal and goad it, while the mistress rode on it. The husband was puzzled why his wife wanted to go find the prophet, because it was not the Sabbath nor was there a new moon—times when he might expect her to look for Elisha. She still did not tell her husband that the child was dead, but simply said, "I want to go." (4:23). Quickly she saddled the ass and told the servant to drive it and to hurry and not delay in doing what she directed.

When she arrived at Mount Carmel, and Elisha saw her approaching, he sent his servant Giezi to meet her and inquire: "Is all well with you, and with your husband, and with your son?" (4:26).

She replied that all was well. However when she came into the presence of Elisha, she threw herself down before him and took hold of his feet. When Giezi came to remove her, the prophet stopped him saying, "Let her alone, for her soul is in anguish, and the Lord has hidden it from me, and has not told me" (4:27). Looking up at Elisha, the sorrowful mother asked: "Did I ask a son of my lord? Did I not say to you, do not deceive me? (4:28). She reminded him that she had not asked for a son, but that it had been Elisha's idea in the first place that she should have one and that she had asked him not to deceive her in the matter.

After hearing what had happened to the boy and considering the situation, Elisha came up with a solution that he presented to Giezi: "Gird up your loins, and take my staff in your hand, and go. If any man meet you, salute him not: and if any man salute you, answer him not, and lay my staff upon the face of the child." Although Giezi left to do as Elisha instructed him, the mother refused to leave Elisha, saying: "As the Lord lives, and as your soul lives, I will not leave you."

Seeing her determination, Elisha set out on the road with the mother back to her home. Giezi, having done as he was directed with no results after he had laid the staff on the face of the child, came to meet Elisha and the mother on their way to her home. Sadly Giezi reported to the prophet: "The child is not risen."

Elisha, entering the room that had been set aside for him, found the lifeless child on his bed. He shut the door, closing out the mother, and began to pray to the Lord. In a manner similar to the way Elijah healed the son of the widow of Sarephta of the Sidonians, Elisha lay down upon the child, put his mouth on the child's, his eyes upon the child's, and his hands upon the child's hands. The child's body began to grow warm. Finally after ministering in this way a number of times, the child began to gasp for breath. Then he opened his eyes.

Elisha directed Giezi to summon the mother. When she entered the room where the child lay, he said, "Take up your son." She fell at the feet of the prophet of God and worshipped the Lord. Then she took up her son, and left (4:37).

We notice when the mother first met Elisha, hoping for a blessing, she invited him to stay in a room in her house. However, when he told her she would have a son, she was incredulous and asked him not to deceive her. But after she, in fact, did give birth to a son, she had great faith in the prophet. When the child succumbed to what appears to be heat prostration or a stroke caused by the heat, she did not panic. She did not even tell her husband that the boy was lifeless. Instead, she went at once to find Elisha. When he asked, through Giezi, how her husband and son were, she simply replied, "Well." When the prophet of God approached her, he immediately perceived the anguish of her soul. She recalled to him his promise that she would have a son. Now she had great faith that the power of God working through His prophet would restore the boy to her. Her faith did not waver, even when Giezi reported that the child was still lifeless, after he had placed Elisha's staff on him. In faith, she turned the child over to Elisha and left him in his care, believing God for his healing. When the boy revived, she worshiped God at the feet of His prophet, and received with thanksgiving the healing that had been given.

If we want to be healed, we must have faith like this woman who did not accept the apparent hopeless condition of her child, but had faith and hope in the power of God to restore him. We must do as this woman did and as St. James tells us:

> Is any man sick among you? Let him bring in the priests of the church, and let them pray over him, anointing him with oil in the name of the Lord. And the

prayer of faith shall save the sick man, and the Lord shall raise him up, and if he be in sins, they shall be forgiven him. (Jm 5: 14–15)

The Apostle James, however, says we have to have faith without wavering, if we want our prayer answered, because if we waver, we are like a wave on the sea that the wind blows hither and yon (1:6). When we receive our healing with thanksgiving, we worship God.

The psalmist is also well acquainted with the healing power of God. He sings to the Lord:

> I will extol You, O Lord, for You have upheld me and have not made my enemies to rejoice over me.
>
> O Lord my God, I have cried to You, and You have healed me. You have brought forth, O Lord, my soul from hell: You have saved me from them that go down into the pit.
>
> Sing to the Lord, O you His saints, and give praise to the memory of his holiness. For wrath is in his indignation, and life in his good will. In the evening weeping shall have place, and in the morning gladness. (29: 2–6)

In this psalm we are to understand that we find life in doing God's will. He heals those who keep His will and cry out for Him to heal them. The proper response to His healing is praise.

Psalm ninety says that because we have made God our habitation no evil shall befall us, and no plague shall come near our dwelling (10). In psalm one hundred and two the psalmist praises God who heals us.

> Bless the Lord, O my soul, and never forget all He has done for you—who forgives all your iniquities, who heals all your diseases, who redeems your life from destruction, who crowns you with mercy and compassion. (2–4)

The relationship between healing and praise is again pinpointed in Psalm 106.

> And they cried to the Lord in their affliction, and He delivered them out of their distresses. He sent His word, and healed them, and delivered them from their destructions. Let the mercies of the Lord give glory to Him, and His wonderful works to the children of men. And let them sacrifice the sacrifice of praise, and declare His works with joy. (106: 19–22)

We, too, must praise God for the healings that He sends us and give glory to Him for all His works, telling our friends and neighbors of the great things God does for us. We are to attend to God's words of wisdom and keep them ever in our hearts, "for they are life to those that find them, and health to all flesh" (Pr 4: 22). We must have a lively faith that God wants to bless and will bless us. We must absolutely believe the word of God and let supernatural faith take possession of our hearts. We must believe God when in His word He says, "who His own self bore our sins in His body upon the tree, that we, having died unto sins, might live unto righteousness, by whose stripes you were healed (I Pe 2:24). Furthermore, we need a proper understanding of just what faith is, because our spiritual life cannot operate without it, and therefore we cannot be healed without faith. The Holy Scripture tells us that "faith is the assurance of [things] hoped for, a conviction of things not seen" (Heb 11:1). By faith we take possession of the good things God wants us to receive. "Without faith it is impossible to be well-pleasing [unto Him], for he that comes to God must believe that He is, and [that] He is a rewarder of them that seek after Him" (Heb 11:6).

Faith speaks to us of the spiritual realities we cannot see and convinces us they are real. We also need faith to believe that God will supply all our needs according to His riches in glory, as the Scripture tells us (Ph 4:19). For Him to supply everything we lack, including health and healing, we have to believe His Word. He has the abundance of all that exists to provide for our necessities. He will meet all our needs—emotional, financial, physical, and spiritual. If we are ill, He has healing waters, but we have to learn how to receive from God and drink the waters he offers us. Some people say that they will be healed some day or when God wishes, or even if God wills it. Healing has already been given us; all we have to do is receive it. The Apostle Peter says "by whose stripes you were healed" (I Pe 2:24). Our healing has already been accomplished by Jesus; all we have to do is to receive it

Why is it so difficult for some people to receive God's gifts? Is it because they do not have the simplicity of little children. When children are offered gifts, they take them willingly and eagerly. It is only world-weary adults that say, "I am not worthy. I don't deserve it." Children demonstrate faith so much more readily that adults. If we have faith, the invisible starts to become visible; the good things of the Lord are poured out on us. Most of us do not live by faith. Rather, we live based upon what our past experiences tell us. Let us become as little children and receive all that God has to give us. We need to open our spiritual eyes with the virtue of faith and perceive the reality our physical eyes cannot see.

Furthermore, if we are seeking a healing from God, we need to get rid of all sin in our life. We cannot be like the psalmist who cries out to God: "There is no health in my flesh, because of Your wrath; there is no peace for my bones, because of my sins" (Ps 37:4). We need to go boldly to the throne of grace. We must confess our sins and let God forgive us, forgive ourselves, and forgive all who have injured us in any way. Then we shall be ready to receive the healing the Lord wishes us to have. We should not be worried about anything, but in everything, by prayer and thanksgiving we should let our petitions be known to God (Ph 4:6).

If we want to be healed, we must sincerely desire healing. Unfortunately there are some people who prefer to hold on to their illness. Perhaps they use it as a crutch, as a way of getting sympathy from others, or as a way of avoiding things they consider to be unpleasant. In order to be well, we must desire to be well with our whole hearts.

While it is good to pray for one's healing, it is far better to have someone pray for us. Healing prayers offered by someone else are more effective than our own. It is especially effective when someone prays for us, while laying their hands on us. The Spirit of the Lord who dwells in faithful believers reaches out with His healing touch to those in need.

We should also avail ourselves of the Sacrament of the Anointing of the Sick that we can receive in the time of serious illness or in advanced old age. In this sacrament, the priest prays for a recovery of health for both body and soul. We must always remember that we are composites of body and soul, and that just as our bodies will share in the glory of the resurrection in the life of the world to come, even now they are to share in the good things of the Lord and experience His peace and freedom from sickness and disease.

"Heavenly Father, we thank You that You are our healer and that You sent Jesus to heal us by his stripes. We accept Your healing, Lord Jesus, with grateful hearts. Holy Spirit, Lord and Giver of Life, fill us with the healing power of God. We praise You Holy Trinity for our healing and give You all the glory. Amen."

10

Peace of Soul

"Peace be to you!" Jesus greeted his apostles on Easter evening when he suddenly appeared in their midst. To convince them that it was truly their Lord, Jesus stretched forth his nail-scarred hands and revealed to them the scarred wound in His side. As they rejoiced in His presence, He again said, "Peace be to you." Then He added, "As the Father has sent me, I also send you." When He had said this, He breathed on them; and said to them: "Receive the Holy Ghost. Whose sins you shall forgive, they are forgiven them; and whose sins you shall retain, they are retained" (Jn 20:2–23).

Throughout the Old Testament, the Holy Spirit is known as the breath of God. So at this time, shortly after His glorious resurrection, Jesus breathes on His apostles and gives them the Spirit, so that they can forgive sins. For just as the Father has sent Jesus, He sends forth his apostles. It was to save people from their sins, that Jesus was born. The angel even told this to Joseph in a dream, when he explained to him that the child born of Mary was to be called Jesus, "For he shall save his people from their sins" (Mt 1:21).

At one point in His public ministry, a man suffering from palsy was brought to Jesus who had just returned to Capernaum. Word got out that He was there, most likely at the house of Simon Peter, and large crowds began to gather at the house, crowding around the entrance door. Four men appeared on the scene carrying a litter on which lay a man suffering from palsy. The man was probably shaking and trembling from his ailment, which causes paralysis of part of the body. He also had probably prevailed upon his four friends to bring him to Jesus, hoping to be cured, knowing that He cured many people.

When the four found it impossible to get in the door of the house, so as to enter the presence of Jesus with the palsied man, they decided to climb up on the roof. Picture them first lifting the empty litter to the roof and then the four of them lifting the paralyzed man up. Somehow they contrived to open up the tiles of the roof and lower the man down into the room where Jesus was. Obviously

Jesus was impressed by the intense faith of these people for going to such great lengths to come to Him. Compassionately, Jesus spoke to the afflicted man, saying "Be of good heart, son, your sins are forgiven you" (Mt 8:2).

When they heard Him say this, some Scribes and Pharisees who were present began thinking that Jesus was speaking blasphemy, because no one but God can forgive sins. Reading their hearts with perfect clarity, Jesus asked them, "What is it you think in your hearts?" Nor waiting for them to reply, he asked them a second question. "Which is easier to say, 'Your sins are forgiven you,' or to say, 'Arise and walk?'" (Lk 5:22–23). When they did not answer, He continued by explaining that in order that they might know that He had power to forgive sins, he will say to the paralyzed man, "Arise, take up your bed, and go into your house." We can only imagine the joy with which the man jumped from his litter, picked it up, and carried it home. It was an occasion of great peace and joy.

The people who witnessed this scene were amazed and full of wonder that a man who resembled them was able to forgive sin, as He proved by His healing the man of palsy. Because of His Easter gift to the Church in which Jesus told the apostles to forgive sins or to retain them, the Church has exercised this ministry in the confessional ever since.

The man with palsy encountered Jesus and found peace, healing, and forgiveness, and went joyfully home glorifying God. That is exactly what each us should experience in the Sacrament of Reconciliation. We should encounter the Savior and His redeeming, forgiving, and healing love. Filled with His peace we should then return home glorifying God with the joy of His salvation filling our hearts.

On another occasion, we see our Lord dealing with a penitent, when he was having dinner in the home of a Pharisee. A certain unnamed woman, known to be a sinner, slipped into the Pharisee's house and stood behind Jesus who was reclining at the table with his feet stretched out behind him. Her tears fell on Jesus' feet, and she wiped them away with her long flowing hair. Humbly she kissed his feet and anointed them with costly ointment from an alabaster box.

As he watched this, the Pharisee was thinking to himself that if Jesus were a prophet, he would know what kind of woman was ministering to him. Reading his thoughts, Jesus told him: "Simon, I have somewhat to say to you" (Lk 7:40). To which the Pharisee replied, "Master, say it."

Jesus proceeded to tell him a story about a certain creditor who had two debtors. One of them owed him ten times as much as the other. Since neither one of them had any money to pay their debts, the creditor cancelled their debts. "Which therefore of the two loves him most? Jesus asked.

Simon replied without hesitation: "I suppose that, he to whom he forgave most" (Lk 7:43).

"You have judged rightly," Jesus told him. Then applying the story of the two debtors to the woman who was still anointing his feet, he explained: "Many sins are forgiven her, because she has loved much. But to whom less is forgiven, he loves less" (Lk 7:47). Then addressing the woman, Jesus told her, "Your sins are forgiven you. Your faith has made you safe, go in peace" (Lk 7:50).

Once again we see how Jesus deals with penitents, giving them peace and joy. He is the merciful Savior whose love endures forever. He is not a legalist, demanding an exact accounting of every sin, but a loving Redeemer who extends the mercy of God to the contrite heart.

When we approach the Sacrament of Reconciliation, we must first examine ourselves on love, for love of God is the first and greatest commandment, and the love of neighbor is the second. The Lord looks for generous souls who embrace His law of love, not legalistic ones who are trying to do the minimum to slip into purgatory. When He finds those who serve Him with loving hearts, he blesses them abundantly. We should approach Him with adoration and give Him the alabaster box of our praise. If we come to Him in faith, He will be pleased with us and grant us His peace and joy.

Today many people have apparently lost the sense of sin. According to Pope Pius XII in a Radio message October 26, 1946, "the sin of the century is the loss of the sense of sin." People fail to realize that we are all part of the mystical body of Christ and that every unloving act affects that body and all of humanity. In his post-synodal apostolic exhortation, "Reconciliation and Penance," John Paul II comments on this effect of sin.

> By virtue of human solidarity which is as mysterious and intangible as it is real and concrete, each individual's sin in some way affects others. This is the other aspect of that solidarity which on the religious level is developed in the profound and magnificent mystery of the communion of saints, thanks to which it has been possible to say that "every soul that rises above itself, raises up the world." To this law of ascent there unfortunately corresponds the law of descent. Consequently one can speak of a communion of sin, whereby a soul that lowers itself through sin drags down with itself the Church and, in some way, the whole world. In other words, there is no sin, not even the most intimate and secret one, the most strictly individual one, that exclusively concerns the person committing it. (16)

In the Sacrament of Reconciliation, we try to undo the shattering of our relationships and to break lose from that "law of descent" and rise above ourselves and try to raise up our little corner of the universe. So as we examine our consciences to prepare for the confession of our sins, we should consider in what way we have damaged the relationships we have with others. We need to consider the things we have left undone that we ought to have done. We should ask ourselves in what ways have we contributed also to social injustice. Have we been prejudiced against other ethnic groups? Have we used ethnic slurs in our speech or have we denigrated anyone by what we have said? Have we failed to contribute to society by giving freely of our talents and some of our treasure? As St. John says how can we love God whom we have not seen, if we do not love our brother whom we have seen? One of the greatest ways to show our love for God is by loving other people.

Fortunately today, confession is not the juridical process it once was in which a confessor felt obliged to ask the penitent probing questions, so that he could, as a judge, assess the person's guilt. Today we are more concerned with a person's total response to Jesus Christ's gospel of love, rather than a meticulous accounting of peccadilloes. What we must try to overcome is our innate selfishness, which is ours due to the weight of original sin that we all share. We will not confess I lied three times, but rather "I lied because I was not generous with my time and did not want to be bothered helping someone." Or perhaps, "I lied because I did not want to see that person." All sin must be viewed in the effects it has on others, not just ourselves. We must strive to grow in love of neighbor. One of the surest signs that we are on the way to heaven is the love we have for our brothers and sisters in Christ. Our Lord himself tells us that whatever we do to the least of our brethren we do unto Him. If we give a cup of cold water in His name, He rewards us for it.

If a student knows the questions that will appear on his final exam, he will prepare the proper answers. We know what the questions will be to get into heaven. Jesus tells us in His own words:

> Then shall the king say to them that shall be on his right hand: Come, you blessed of my Father, possess you the kingdom prepared for you from the foundation of the world. For I was hungry, and you gave me to eat; I was thirsty, and you gave me to drink; I was a stranger, and you took me in; naked, and you covered me; sick, and you visited me. I was in prison, and you came to me. Then shall the just answer him, saying: Lord, when did we see you hungry, and fed you; thirsty, and gave you drink? And when did we see you a stranger, and took you in? Or naked, and covered you? Or when did we

see you sick or in prison, and came to you? And the king answering shall say to them: Amen, I say to you, as long as you did it to one of these my least brethren, you did it to me. (Mt 26:34–40)

To those people who do not do all these things, he will say "Depart from me, you cursed, into everlasting fire which was prepared for the devil and his angels" (Mt 25:41). They shall go into everlasting punishment, but the just will go into life everlasting. Today many people say they do not believe in the existence of hell. Jesus says it exists. Whom are we going to believe?

When we approach the Sacrament of Reconciliation, we should be seeking an encounter with Christ, for it is He who ministers to us through the ministry of the priest who is dispensing Christ's Easter gift of peace. We should always remember that we are celebrating the Church's liturgy and make it an occasion of praising God and rejoicing in His love. We must always expect his peace and joy to flow into us with the words of absolution. This sacrament lends itself to the praise of the glory of His grace. It is a time when both priest and penitent can glorify God with their faith in His promises of salvation and forgiveness.

The Sacrament of Reconciliation is the great sacrament of peace. It applies the peace of Christ to each one of us individually. We in turn should take that peace home with us and share it with all those we encounter in our daily lives.

Dear Lord Jesus, we thank you for your Easter gift to your Church—the forgiveness of sins. We want to examine our lives according to Your teachings in the gospels. When we find we do not accomplish all that You wish for us, we will repent and try harder to grow in Your love and in the love of our neighbor. And as for the past, we will do like St. Paul who says: "But one thing I do—forgetting the things that are behind, and stretching forth myself to those that are before, I press towards the mark, to the prize of the supernal vocation of God in Christ Jesus" (Ph 2:13–14). We will forget the past and press on, growing in the love of God and neighbor, until we come to that perfect and endless day of eternity. Amen."

11

Peace from Feelings

To have true and lasting peace we must learn to control our feelings. There are so many things in life that we just do not want to do. No one wants to carry out the garbage after dinner, yet if we want to get rid of it, we have to pack it up and take it out. In almost every household from the wealthiest to the poorest, the man of the house carries it out. If we want a clean car, we have to wash it, even if we do not feel like doing it. If we want peace, we have to learn how to live in peace. This means controlling our feelings and emotions. We must take control of them and not let them dominate us.

Anger, greed, sloth, lust, pride, gluttony, envy—these are the things that can steal our peace, if we do not learn how to control them. They have been called the seven deadly sins for centuries, and they can be very deadly, if they get out of hand. Because of original sin, we all have a proclivity to yield to them all.

When we yield to anger, our peace deserts us. Anger if unchecked can lead to hatred and even murder. At the very least, it can be responsible for our imperfections, when we yield to it, and become impatient and lose our peace. We need to eradicate the first stirring of it in our hearts. The more often we try to conquer it, the easier it becomes to keep it under control.

Some people use simple little devices to help eradicate anger. Some count to ten before acting on their emotions. Others might hold their breath a few seconds. The best thing to do, however, is pray. A quick prayer asking the Lord to help stop the stirrings of anger in our hearts is very effective. And then if we still succumb to anger, we can make ourselves do some penance to help enforce our desire not to lose our composure. The most important thing is to continue to work on it and, with the passing of time we will find that we are not losing our peace, as often as we formerly did. The result will be a more peaceful and tranquil life for ourselves and those around us.

It is said that the young are troubled by lust, people in the prime of life, by pride and the desire for power, and the elderly by greed. It seems to be a tendency among the elderly to hold on to their possessions and to amass more if possible, as if worldly goods were a buffer against death. We all know that shrouds do not have pockets. Jesus tells us that we are not to lay up treasures on earth where rust and moth destroy them or thieves steal them, but to lay up treasures in heaven, because there they are incorruptible, and where our treasure is there also our hearts will be (Mt:19–20).

The Lord also told a parable about a certain rich man whose lands produced a lot of fruit—so much fruit that he had nowhere to store it. The man asked himself: "What shall I do, because I have no room where to bestow my fruits?" (Lk 12:17). He decided to pull down his old barns that were too small and limited in their capacity and build new and bigger ones, saying: "This will I do. I will pull down my barns, and will build greater, and into them will I gather all things that are grown to me, and my goods. And I will say to my soul, 'Soul, you have much good laid up for many years, take your rest—eat, drink, and make good cheer'" (Lk 12:18).

What happened to the man and his stored up treasure? The Lord concludes the parable, by quoting what God had to say to the rich man: "You fool, this night do they require your soul of you, and whose shall those things be which you have provided?" And Jesus ends the story by saying "So is he that lays up treasure for himself, and is not rich towards God" (Lk 12:21).

No matter what our age, we need to practice laying up treasures in heaven, so that when we are old, greed will not be able to entrap us in its deadly snares.

As for sloth—people of any age can succumb to it. Most of us think of it rather as laziness, for sloth is not part of our normal everyday vocabulary, but we all know what it means to be lazy. There are so many chores that have to be done, and we would rather just forget about them. However, if we are lazy and negligent about doing the little things that need to be done, we will have greater trouble in dealing with larger issues. We are all touched by laziness from time to time, but if we do not control our tendencies to be lazy, we can fall into serious sin, by neglecting to deal with the important issues of life. Sloth can destroy the Divine Life in our souls.

None of the seven deadly sins rarely attaches to an individual without bringing with it the rest of them. We recall that Jesus cast the seven devils out of Mary Magdalen, and she became a great saint and the one that He chose to send word to His apostles that He is risen (Lk 8:2, Mr 16:9). For an excellent study of the effects of the seven deadly sins, let us consider the Herodians, a family plagued with strife, brawling, murders, envy, greed, gluttony, and lust, including incest, who were in power at the time of the birth of Jesus, at His crucifixion, and during the early years of the nascent Church.

When Jesus was born in Bethlehem, old Herod the Great, called great because of his power, not his virtue, heard that wise men from the East were looking for the One who had been born King of the Jews, for they had seen His star in the East and had come to worship Him. Herod, a crafty old fox, always alert for anyone or anything that might diminish his power and threaten his rule, met with the wise men in an attempt to learn the whereabouts of Jesus so that he could destroy Him, a helpless infant. After inquiring as to where they had seen the star, he told them to go find the child and then return to him and let him know where the child was so he too could go and adore Him.

God in His Loving Providence protected the newborn king. After they found the infant Jesus and presented Him with their gifts, a dream came to the wise men, or magi as they are also called, instructing them not to return to Herod. When an angel of the Lord appeared to Joseph in a dream, he gave him the following instructions: "Arise, and take the child and his mother, and fly into Egypt, and be there until I shall tell you. For it will come to pass that Herod will seek the child to destroy Him" (Mt 2:13).

Joseph got up right away that very night and left at once for Egypt with Mary and Jesus. Furious that the wise men had not followed his instructions, Herod sent men to kill all male children under the age of two in Bethlehem and the surrounding area (Mt. 2:16). This wanton and brutal act of destruction characterizes Herod and his family.

The Herodians were not a Jewish family, rather they were Idumeans who were conquered by John Hyrcanus in 125 BC, forcibly circumcised, and incorporated into the Asmonean kingdom, but ever antagonistic to it. Strife existed constantly and continually between the Asmoneans and the Herodians. The Asmonean Antigonus captured Jerusalem where Phasael, Herod's brother was governor. As a result, Phasael committed suicide by dashing his brains out against the prison walls where he was confined. Antigonus, who captured his brother Hyrcanus, at the same time, made his brother incapable of ever holding priestly office, by chopping off his ears. At the same time, Herod was in Rome where he persuaded Antony and Augustus to give him the crown of Judea in 37 BC. In 41 BC, Antony appointed Herod tetrarch of Judea.

Herod began his reign by trying utterly to exterminate the Asmonean dynasty, also known as the Maccabees. Although he was married to one of them, Mariamme, the granddaughter of Hyrcanus, he did not spare her and had her put to death, together with her mother Alexandra. He had his wife the only person, it seems, that he ever loved, slain instantly in a fit of jealous rage. Her brother Aristobulus, he had drowned after enticing him to go for a swim at Jericho. Finally, shortly, before his own death, he executed his sons by Mariamme. In short, he was a monster and a tyrant.

When Herod named Antipater, his son by Doris, his first wife, as his heir to the throne, this son became impatient to wield power and tried to poison his father, but the plot failed, because Herod's brother Pheroras drank the poison instead. Old Herod threw Antipater into prison, later executed him, and made his youngest son, Antipas, his heir. Herod died five days after the execution of Antipater. Provoked by jealousy and rage, Herod, when his body was consumed with loathsome disease, and he knew that his death was immanent, ordered many prominent people thrown in prison, and commanded that they should all be killed just as soon as he died, so that there would be mourning in the land upon his passing.

Pride, greed, envy, and lust for power were not Herod's only vices. He married ten times and had nine wives at the same time. Risking the wrath of Antony, he even had a child by Cleopatra. There are few families that are as dysfunctional and immoral as the Herodians who intermarried, giving the student of history a difficult time in trying to sort out their relationships. A case in point is that of Herod's son Antipas who was tetrarch of Galilee and Peraea from the death of Herod the Great in 4 BC until 39 AD. Because his mother was a Samaritan, named Malthace, and his father Idumean, he did not have any Jewish blood at all. Having been educated in Rome, he picked up Roman customs, culture, and vices, which were, of course, pagan.

Antipas first married a daughter of Aretas king of Arabia from the rose city of Petra. When he met Herodias, the wife of his brother Philip, at Rome, he promptly seduced her, sending his wife back to her father. Not only was Herodias the wife of his half-brother Philip, she was also the daughter of another half-brother Aristobulus, making her his niece. Therefore his union with Herodias was twice sinful, according to Jewish law. Later, when the couple went to live in Jerusalem, taking with them Salome, Herodias' and Philip's daughter, Antipas' lust got him involved in the murder of St. John the Baptist, because he became intoxicated by the voluptuous dancing of Salome.

Because John had preached in the desert, saying that it was wrong for Antipas to be married to his brother's wife, Herodias, in the tradition of her blood-thirsty grandfather Herod the Great, longed for his death. She prevailed upon her husband to arrest John and throw him into prison, but was unable to convince him to kill the prophet of God. Instead, she took advantage of her husband's weaknesses to accomplish her steadfast purpose to get rid of John, when she had the occasion.

The moment she had been waiting for came when, to celebrate his birthday, Antipas held a large supper party for the princes, tribunes, and chief men of Galilee (Mr 6:21). At the gala event, Salome danced to entertain the guests. Anyone who has ever traveled in the Middle East knows that the Oriental dance of the region is the belly dance in which a woman bares her body and undulates in seductive ways. No doubt Antipas was well plied with wine and stuffed with food, as he gazed upon her, when she whirled and twirled to incite the lust of the male viewers. In a burst of enthusiasm, Herod said to the girl: "Ask of me what you will, and I will give it to you" (Mr 6:22). Then he swore that he would do it. "Whatsoever you shall ask, I will give you, though it be the half of my kingdom."

Pleased with her success, Salome went to her mother Herodias, and inquired: "What shall I ask?"

The girl could have asked for wealth, jewels, all manner of things to delight her. The mother coldly hissed: "The head of John the Baptist!" (Mr 6:24).

Returning to the banquet, Salome approached Antipas and said: "I will that forthwith you give me in a dish, the head of John the Baptist!" (Mr 6:26).

Having made an oath in front of his guests that he would give the girl what she requested, he sent an executioner immediately to behead John and to return with his head in a dish. He was Herodian through and through. Old Herod the Great would probably have been proud of him and Herodias. Legend has it that she thrust a sharp hairpin through the tongue that had offended her.

Antipas is the Herod to whom Pilate sent Jesus, when the multitudes accused Him before the Roman ruler of Jerusalem (Lk 23:1). Wanting to avoid dealing with Jesus, Pilate, upon learning that He was a Galilean and knowing that Antipas was in the city for the Passover, sent Him to him. Antipas was glad to see Jesus, Holy Scripture tells us, because he had heard a lot about Him and was hoping to see Him work a miracle for his amusement. Although he questioned Jesus at length, the Lord of Glory did not answer him anything—not a word. All the while, the chief priests and the scribes were continually accusing Him to Antipas. Not being able to get Him to talk to them, Antipas and his soldiers mocked Jesus and considered Him to be of no account, and putting a white robe on him, sent Him back to Pilate.

Antipas, Herodias, and Salome all came to a sad end. In time, the Roman Senate banished Herodias and Antipas to Lyons, because Herodius, jealous of her brother Agrippa, goaded her husband into demanding that Emperor Caligula grant him the title of king. Banished to Lyons, they suffered greatly and died miserably. It is recounted that Salome, while walking across ice on a frozen body of water, fell into the water, when the ice broke. She fell in such a way that her head was caught on the ice while her body dangled in the water. The ice was so sharp that it almost severed her head, ironically causing her to die by decapitation, the same pain that she had inflicted on John the Baptist.

We have still not heard the last of the Herodians. Unfortunately, there is more to tell of their unsavory deeds. When a family gets enmeshed in the deadly sins, they have a way of continuing generation after generation.

When Antipas and Herodias were exiled to Lyons, the territories ruled over by Antipas, as well as all his property, went to Herodias' brother Agrippa I, because he had curried the favor of Caligula. When Claudius became emperor, Agrippa I also got in good standing with him so that he increased his territory by adding Judea and Samaria to his domain.

Agrippa I was the grandson of Herod the Great and the son of Aristobulus and Bernice and a true Herodian, but he also carried Asmonean blood. He persecuted the Christian Church in an attempt to gain support of the Jews. The most dastardly thing he did was to arrest and kill the Apostle James, the brother of John, with a sword in 42 AD.

Seeing how much the death of James pleased the Jews, Agrippa arrested the Apostle Peter and put him in prison. However, the Lord rescued Peter, for He had much more for Him to do before calling him home.

Agrippa I did not have any better ending than did his sister Herodias. In 33 AD, he went to Caesarea to a public event at which he appeared wearing a robe of silver that really glistened in the morning sunlight. He made such a striking appearance in the silver robe that people began calling him a "god," and he did not refute their flattery. Suddenly he was stricken with abdominal pain that was excruciating and had to be removed to bed. He died several days later. Holy Scripture speaking of this event says: "And forthwith an angel of the Lord struck him, because he had not given the honor to God, and being eaten up by worms, he gave up the ghost" (Ac 12:23).

St. Paul also had an encounter with the Herodians, when he was in prison at Caesarea, and Festus wanted him to return to Jerusalem and stand trial. Paul refused and invoked his right as a Roman citizen to go to Rome and have his case heard there by Caesar (Ac 25:11). Shortly thereafter, Agrippa II and Bernice came to Caesarea and heard about Paul who was waiting to go to Rome. Agrippa said to Festus "I would also hear the man, myself" (Ac 25:22).

"You shall hear him" Festus replied.

The next day Agrippa and Bernice came with great pomp into the chamber where the audience was to be held, together with the tribunes and the principal men of the city. Festus explained that he could find no fault with Paul, but since he had appealed to Caesar, he would send him to Rome. He requested King Agrippa to examine him and help him decide what to tell Rome about Paul.

Turning to Paul, Agrippa said "Paul, You are permitted to speak for yourself."

Paul proceeded to relate to Agrippa the events of His life, including the vision He had of Jesus on the Road to Damascus, and of how Jesus rose from the dead. After presenting the testimony of His faith in Christ, Paul asked Agrippa: "Do you believe the prophets, O King Agrippa? I know you believe" (Ac 26:27).

Agrippa replied, "Paul in a little you are persuading me to become a Christian (Ac 26:29).

In conclusion, Agrippa told Festus that he could find nothing wrong with Paul: "This man might have been set at liberty, if he had not appealed to Caesar" (Ac 26:32).

Who were Agrippa II and Bernice? They were brother and sister—the children of Agrippa I and Cypros. They also had a beautiful sister Drusilla that left her husband Azizus to marry Felix, the procurator of Judea who was intoxicated by her beauty and persuaded her to marry him. They had a son named Agrippa who perished in the eruption of Vesuvius.

Agrippa II was educated in Rome in the emperor's palace. Emperor Claudius in 50 AD made him king of Chalcis, a part of the Lebanon. He controlled the temple treasury and was the person who appointed the Jewish high priest. For these reasons, the Romans discussed Jewish religious affairs with him. Most probably, Festus asked him to listen to Paul at Caesarea, because of his position in Jewish religious matters. In 52 AD, Claudius extended his domain by giving him the old tetrarchies of Philip and Lysanius. In 55 AD, Nero gave him additional territory.

Bernice, the sister of Agrippa II, was born about 28 AD. When she was thirteen years old, she married a man called Marcus who was the son of a Jewish official named Alexander. When her husband died, her father, Agrippa I, arranged for her to marry his brother Herod of Chalcis, who was, of course, her uncle. Bernice gave birth to two sons before he died in 48 AD. Thereafter, she lived in an incestuous relationship with her brother Agrippa II. Although she married Polemo, the king of Celicia, she left him to return to Agrippa II. She made an appeal to the insane Roman Procurator Gessius Florus in AD 66 not to ransack the temple in Jerusalem, but he did not listen to her. When war broke out and the Jewish rebels burned their palaces, she stood side by side with Agrippa II.

Agrippa II warned the Jews not to resist the Romans, because he knew it was sheer futility to do so. During the war, he fought with the Romans and was injured by a stone slung at him at the siege of Gamala. When Jerusalem and the nation were destroyed, Agrippa II and Bernice moved to Rome, where she engaged in scandalous sexual activity with Vespasian and Titus, father and son. Agrippa II, the last of the Herodians, died in the year 100 AD.

Anger, greed, sloth, lust, pride, gluttony, envy—all seven of the deadly sins consumed the Herodians. In the story of this family, we can see the devastating effects of sin. Most of us will never get as deeply involved with the seven deadly sins as did the Herodians, but even a little bit of them can rob us of our peace. Envy and peace cannot dwell in the same mind, heart, and soul. Envy is poison to the person who yields to it, as are the other six of these deadly sins. We must always be on guard against them and nip them in the bud, if we feel them stirring within us. Otherwise we will have no peace and our lives will become tormented and destroyed.

We have to learn to control our feelings, and say no to our desires when they are unreasonable. We must be guided by our reason and not our emotions. When we are young, it is difficult to control our feelings, but with practice it becomes easier as we mature. If we learn to control our desires and our feelings, we will know great peace of soul.

We learn to take control of our lives by asking the Holy Spirit to give us wisdom and knowledge and to fill us with all his gifts and charisms. The Holy Spirit cannot live in a soul that is dominated by passion and the emotions. Let us invite Him to take possession of our souls and give us the peace that passes all understanding.

"Sweet Holy Spirit, we ask you to fill us with Your presence and make us like Jesus so that we may receive His gift of peace. We are weary of trying to satisfy all our desires and of giving way to all our emotions. Our desires are insatiable, if we give them free reign. Our unbridled emotions lead us to states of exhaustion. Take control of our lives that we may know the profound peace that comes to those who take You for their Counselor. Amen."

12

Peace without Fear

When fear holds us in its grip, we have no peace. In today's society we suffer from all manner of fears. Just reading the morning paper or listening to the local television report the news of the day can send fear coursing through our bodies, making our hearts beat a bit faster, raising our blood pressure, and giving us a general feeling of anxiety, as we hear information about the latest threats of terrorists to attack us, or the advent of a new and fatal virus or disease, such as SARS that is circling the globe. We are afraid of losing those we love, or of being abandoned by them. We fear the loss of all the material things we have worked so hard to amass. Thoughts of sickness and death haunt us, and with death the possibility of judgment and the fear of hell. How can we have peace, when we are bombarded by such thoughts? Yet down through the centuries the Church has continued to proclaim in its liturgies, *"Pax Domini sit semper vobiscum!* The peace of the Lord be always with you!"

God wants us to have peace, and not be afraid. The most constant greeting in the Holy Scripture is "Fear not!" The story of God's interaction with human beings begins with Abram, before he became Abraham. The book of Genesis tells us that "the word of the Lord came to Abram by a vision, saying: "Fear not, Abram, I am your protector, and your reward exceeding great" (15:1). Still later, the Lord gave a similar message to Isaac, saying: "I am the God of Abraham your father; do not fear, for I am with you. I will bless you, and multiply your seed for my servant Abraham's sake" (Ge 26:24). Continuing to direct His people, the Lord spoke to Jacob: "I am the most mighty God of your father. Fear not; go down into Egypt, for I will make a great nation of you there" (Ge 46:3). In dealing with Moses as the leader of the people, the Lord becomes more explicit in his directions: "Do my precepts, and keep my judgments, and fulfill them that you may dwell in the land without any fear" (Le 25:18).

> If you walk in my precepts, and keep my commandments, and do them, I will give you rain in due seasons. And the ground shall bring forth its increase, and the trees shall be filled with fruit. The threshing of your harvest shall reach unto the vintage, and the vintage shall reach unto the sowing time, and you shall eat your bread to the full, and dwell in your land without fear. I will give peace to your coasts. You shall sleep, and there shall be none to make you afraid. I will take away evil beasts, and the sword shall not pass through your quarters. (Le 26:3–6)

However, if the people do not obey the Lord and keep His commandments, fear will be their portion. We recall that Adam experienced fear, after he and Eve disobeyed God and ate the forbidden fruit. Adam said to God who came looking for him: "I heard Your voice in paradise; and I was afraid, because I was naked, and I hid myself" (Ge 3:10). Thus fear came to Eden and to mankind. Fear is the consequence of sin. As Proverbs teaches: "The wicked man flees, when no man pursues, but the just, bold as a lion, shall be without dread" (Pr 28:1). Adam had been warned what would happen to him, if he disobeyed God. The Lord gave similar warnings to His people, upon giving them the Mosaic Law. He said:

> But if you will not hear me, nor do all my commandments, if you despise my laws, and contemn my judgments so as not to do those things which are appointed by me, and to make void my covenant, I also will do these things to you—I will quickly visit you with poverty, and burning heat, which shall waste your eyes, and consume your lives. You shall sow your seed in vain, which shall be devoured by your enemies. I will set my face against you, and you shall fall down before your enemies, and shall be made subject to them that hate you. You shall flee when no man pursues you. But if you will not, yet for all this, obey me, I will chastise you seven times more for your sins. (Le 26:14–18)

Finally after enumerating all the ills that will befall a disobedient people, the Lord tells them that fear will consume them:

> And as to them that shall remain of you, I will send fear in their hearts in the countries of their enemies, the sound of a flying leaf shall terrify them, and they shall flee as it were from the sword; they shall fall, when no man pursues them. (Le 26:36)

They will suffer from irrational fears; anxiety will destroy their peace. The Lord will give them fearful hearts, and languishing eyes, and souls consumed with pensiveness (De 28:65). And their lives shall be as it were hanging before them.

They shall fear night and day, neither shall they trust their lives (De 28:66). Because of their fearful hearts, they shall be terrified (De 28.67).

But those who are obedient and keep the law of the covenant need not fear enemies. The word of God says: "You shall not fear them, because the Lord your God is in the midst of you, a God mighty and terrible" They are to pass over the Jordan, and dwell in the land the Lord will give them that they "may have rest from all enemies round about and may dwell without any fear" (De 12:10). If they go out to war with enemies and see that they are outnumbered, they are not to fear, because God is with them (De 20:1). "And the Lord who is your leader, He himself will be with you. He will not leave you, nor forsake you. Fear not, neither be dismayed" (De 31:8).

Repeatedly in the Holy Scripture, the Lord tells his people not to fear. After the death of Moses when Joshua became leader of the people of God, the Lord spoke to him as well: "Behold I command you, take courage, and be strong. Fear not and be not dismayed, because the Lord your God is with you in all things" (Jos 1:9). And to Gideon, He spoke these words: "Peace be with you! Fear not, you shall not die" (Jd 6:23).

Fear is a dreadful thing, a paralyzing emotion that makes it difficult for one to act wisely and well. Job's friend Elizphaz the Temanite knows what it is to have great fear. He describes it in this way: "In the horror of a vision by night, when deep sleep is wont to hold men, fear seized upon me, and trembling, and all my bones were affrighted: And when a spirit passed before me, the hair of my flesh stood up" (Jb 4:13–15). No doubt Shakespeare was correct when he penned these lines: "Of all base passions, fear is the most accursed" (*King Henry I.* V.II). The writer of the book of Job also spoke great wisdom when he said "There is no power upon earth that can be compared with him who was made to fear no one" (Jb 41:24).

We must be completely convinced that God does not want His people to fear anything or anyone. We can take great courage and inspiration from the words of the psalmist. If we truly belong to the Lord we can make the words of the psalms ours, and we can stand on their assurances of God's protection and loving care. With David we can say, "I will not fear thousands of the people surrounding me. Arise, O Lord! Save me, O my God" (Ps 3:7). Or we can make the following our own: "For though I should walk in the midst of the shadow of death, I will fear no evils, for You are with me. Your rod and your staff, they have comforted me (Ps 22:4). With David we can ask: "The Lord is my light and my salvation, whom shall I fear? The Lord is the protector of my life, of whom shall I be afraid?" (Ps 26:1).

The psalmist also encourages us to fear the Lord, saying "Fear the Lord, all you his saints, for there is no want to them that fear him (33:10). Here we must observe that fear of the Lord means that we have great reverence for Him, and strive to keep His covenant by observing all He commands. There is no servile fear in the fear of God.

Just what does it mean to fear God? The book of Proverbs gives us many insights into the significance of fearing God. "The fear of the Lord is the beginning of wisdom" (Pr 9:10). "In the fear of the Lord is confidence of strength, and there shall be hope for His children" (Pr 14:26). The fear of the Lord is a "fountain of wisdom" (15:33), "a fountain of life" (14:27) that shall "prolong days" (10:37). In it is found "confidence and strength" (14:26), and by the fear of the Lord men depart from evil (16:16). "The fear of the Lord is unto life, and he [that has it] shall abide in fullness without being visited with evil" (19:23). Finally, "the fruit of humility is the fear of the Lord—riches and glory and life" (22:4).

To fear the Lord is to put a reverential trust in Him that makes us want to do things to please Him and to avoid anything that would displease Him. It is a feeling of reverence for God which is inspired by awe and the fear of punishment, if one disobeys. The psalmist tells us that "Blessed are all they that fear the Lord, that walk in His ways" (126.1). The angel of the Lord encamps around those that fear Him and delivers them (Ps 23:14). So we see that the fear of the Lord is something very desirable for us to attain. Fear of the Lord is a very positive thing.

Another kind of positive fear is the fear we experience when we are under attack, such as when a snake is poised to strike us. Fears of this kind help us to protect ourselves in times of danger. However most of our fears exist only in our own minds. They are phantasms that haunt us and often paralyze us from doing good. Most often the things we fear do not come to pass.

So what do we do with our fears? We put them in the hands of the Lord, believing that He will protect us from all evil. Faith is what we need to deal with fear. Our Lord reproached His apostles for being afraid. One evening when the Lord got in a boat to cross over the Sea of Galilee to the land of the Gerasens, the apostle were with him, when a sudden squall arose on the sea. Natives of the area are quick to explain that the Sea of Galilee can become very rough, when the wind ruffles the waves and piles them high. The storm this day must have been especially severe, because Peter and some of the others who were accustomed to boating on the sea found it very disquieting.

Jesus had had a very busy day surrounded by pressing multitudes of people and was probably very tired, because He fell asleep in the boat, oblivious to the swirling and churning waters. Matthew, the former tax collector, describes the storm as being a "great tempest" and says that "the boat was covered with waves (8:24). Mark says it was "filled" (4:37). We can picture the apostles wondering what to do?

Matthew might have said, "Andrew, you wake him up."

Perhaps Andrew replied, "No, no. You do it, Mathew."

We can imagine Peter coming forth and saying to them both that *he* will wake Him up. He approached Jesus cautiously and then finally yelled so that he could be heard above the wind and the slapping of the waves on the boat. "Lord, save us! We perish!" Master, does it not concern You that we perish?" (Mr 4:38).

Calmly, Jesus, who was sleeping in the back of the boat on a pillow, surveyed them all and asked: "Why are you fearful, O you of little faith?" And Jesus arose, rebuked the wind, and spoke to the sea: "Peace, be still." The wind subsided and the sea became calm (Mr 4:39). Mark, who is recounting Peter's version of this event, comments that they "feared exceedingly." And Jesus said to them: "Why are you fearful? Have you not faith yet?" (Mr 4:40)

On another occasion, Jesus again rebuked His apostles for having little faith and told them not to be solicitous for their lives, or what they would eat, or about their clothing. He reminded them of the providential care the Heavenly Father gives to His creation, how He feed the ravens and clothes the lilies of the field in glory.

> Consider the lilies, how they grow. They labor not, neither do they spin. But I say to you, not even Solomon in all his glory was clothed like one of these. Now if God clothe in this manner the grass that is today in the field, and tomorrow is cast into the oven; how much more you, O you of little faith? (Lk 12:22–28)

Patiently Jesus explains to them that their Heavenly Father knows what they need, and if we seek God's kingdom and His justice, He will provide for all our needs. And as St. Paul says: "May my God supply all your want, according to his riches in glory in Christ Jesus" (Ph 4:19). To console them Jesus affectionately added, "Fear not, little flock, for it has pleased your Father to give you a kingdom (Lk 13:32). Since it has pleased the Father to give us a kingdom, we know he will not give us scorpions when we ask for eggs, or stones, if we ask for bread, or serpents for fish.

Are we people of little faith? Or do we trust God to take care of us in His loving Providence? Do we keep His commandments as He insists we do, if we want

His loving care? Jesus tells us: "If you love me, keep my commandments" (Jn 14:15).

If we keep His commandments and love Him, our fears will vanish like smoke in a windstorm. As the beloved St. John explains, there is no fear in love. Perfect love casts out all fear. We cannot have fear in our hearts, if they are filled with love. If we have fear, it is a sign that our love is not yet perfect. Having perfect love does not mean that we will not feel pain. The love of Jesus for the Heavenly Father was perfection, and no one has greater love for people than He who lay down His life for us. Nevertheless, he recoiled from the pain of crucifixion, as He anguished in Gethsemane the night before He died. But He was fearless, and He carried the cross valiantly and shed every last drop of His blood that we might learn how to love perfectly and have no fear.

"Lord Jesus, make us perfect in love so that all fear will be gone from us. We know that you care for us more than we can possibly imagine. We confide ourselves completely into Your holy hands. We trust you to lead us and guide and keep us close to Your heart, so that when our lives are finished on this earth, You will welcome us home to You. Amen."

13

Peace without Suffering

We experience pain. It is unavoidable, but it can be managed, if we have the right attitudes. If our attitudes are wrong, then our pain causes us great suffering. The trouble is that we agonize and anguish over things that are really of no importance. For example, we desire things that we really do not need, and when we cannot have them, we suffer and lose our interior peace. We have certain expectations about how our lives should be, and when they are not met, we anguish over not having them realized. For example, many women want their sons to become priests, and when they do not, suffering is in the mothers' minds. Their expectations for their sons were not realized, and because of this they lose their peace of soul.

Because of our wrong attitudes, we need to experience circumcision of the heart to live in the peace of Christ without suffering. If we embrace it, the Word of God transforms us radically and makes us into victorious people who can rise above suffering and who can be joyful in spite of pain. We are children of the King, princes and princesses of the kingdom of God. He has chosen us, and has drawn us into His kingdom. Although the rituals and liturgies of the Church are wonderful for expressing our faith, our hearts must be dedicated to Jesus Christ. We must live the Word of God, united to the will of God, or all that we do is worth absolutely nothing. Many people who go to church every Sunday see things only from the viewpoint of the world in which they live and fail to perceive things the way God sees them. There are people in our churches that simply cannot see—they are spiritually blind. Because they have not encountered Jesus, they do not value the Word of God and try to live it daily. They have heard about Jesus, but they don't really know Him.

If we are blind and have not experienced the victorious light of Christ, or perhaps have caught only a small glimpse of it, we will suffer our way though life. Doesn't everyone suffer? No! Is it possible not to suffer? Yes! Everyone has pain, but, by the proper attitudes, anguish and suffering can be avoided. However, we do realize that there are some people who enjoy suffering, but they are masochists and are not psychologically normal. The way normal people regard pain affects the way they experience it, and if they have the right attitudes, they are able to manage it, so that it does not cause them suffering.

Problems arise when we have expectations about the people and things that surround us. We make rules and when they are broken, we suffer. Some women suffer because they are a few pounds overweight, or because they feel their face is not pretty. Some men suffer because they do not excel at sports. They expect to par every hole on the golf course, and, when they do not, they agonize over their game and lose the joy of it. The more unsatisfied desires we have, the more we will anguish and grieve.

To avoid this unnecessary suffering, we must renounce our desires, change our way of looking at things, and submit everything in our lives to the will of God. Until we do this we will not have peace, we will not be happy, and we will continue to suffer. Our plans for our lives are not the same as what God has planned for us, and this causes us to lose peace of soul. Until we learn to put everything into His hands and accept His plan for our lives, we will not be at peace.

Negativity robs us of our peace and makes us suffer. If we don't renounce all negative thoughts from our minds, hearts, and daily life, we will not be happy. Saying such things as "I never get ahead," or "I sacrifice myself all the time" or "People are hypocrites"—all reflect a wrong way of thinking and improper attitudes that will only produce suffering in our lives. We all have problems, it is how we handle them that counts. We all experience the same reality day in and day out, however, what is merely painful to one person causes suffering and anguish in another.

When our faith in God is absolute, we will view life in a peaceful manner, by placing everything in the hands of the Lord. Peace will reign in our hearts, minds, and souls, when we seek first the kingdom of God and His righteousness, knowing, that if we do, all other things will be given to us. When we place all in God's hands, we know that He will safeguard those we love. We will not have to worry about losing them, for our lives will be intertwined with theirs for all eternity. We really possess nothing—all is in the hands of God. The only person who has reason to fear is one who has something to lose. If we have the wrong attitudes, we believe we possess very much—money, cars, houses, spouses, children, and our own bodies. The truth is we really own nothing. It all belongs to God. When we leave this world, we can take nothing with us—nothing except the love that is in our souls.

To avoid suffering and be at peace, we must take absolute control over all our thoughts, desires, and actions. We are responsible for everything we think, desire, and do. As St. John Cassian explains:

> It is impossible for the mind not to be approached by thoughts, but it is in the power of every earnest man either to admit them or to reject them. As then their rising up does not entirely depend on ourselves, so the rejection or admission of them lies in our own power. But because we said that it is impossible for the mind not to be approached by thoughts, you must not lay everything to the charge of the assault, or to those spirits who strive to instil them into us, else there would not remain any free will in man, nor would efforts for our improvement be in our power, but it is, I say, to a great extent in our power to improve the character of our thoughts and to let either holy and spiritual thoughts or earthly ones grow up in our hearts. (XVII)

If we control our thoughts, desires, and actions, nothing or no one can make us unhappy or rob us of our peace, as long as we do not permit it.

St John Chrysostom wrote a very persuasive treatise titled "No One Can Harm the Man Who Does Not Harm Himself." He says:

> We have the common assumption of mankind, which in the course of ages has taken deep root in the minds of the multitude and declaims to the following effect throughout the world. All things, it says, have been turned upside down. The human race is full of much confusion, and many are they who every day are being wronged, insulted, subjected to violence and injury, the weak by the strong, the poor by the rich: and as it is impossible to number the waves of the sea, so is it impossible to reckon the multitude of those who are the victims of intrigue, insult, and suffering; and neither the correction of law, nor the fear of being brought to trial, nor anything else can arrest this pestilence and disorder, but the evil is increasing every day, and the groans, and lamentations, and weeping of the sufferers are universal; and the judges who are appointed to reform such evils, themselves intensify the tempest, and inflame the disorder, and hence many of the more senseless and despicable kind, seized with a new kind of frenzy, accuse the providence of God, when they see the forbearing man often violently seized, racked, and oppressed, and the audacious, impetuous, low and low-born man waxing rich, and invested with authority, and becoming formidable to many, and inflicting countless troubles upon the more moderate, and this perpetrated both in town and country, and desert, on sea and land.

Nevertheless, the saint protests that it is those who do evil to others that are the ones who are injured—for they injure themselves.

For it is not stress of circumstances, nor variation of seasons, nor insults of men in power, nor intrigues besetting thee like snow storms, nor a crowd of calamities, nor a promiscuous collection of all the ills to which mankind is subject, which can disturb even slightly the man who is brave, and temperate, and watchful; just as on the contrary the indolent and supine man who is his own betrayer cannot be made better, even with the aid of innumerable ministrations.

He concludes by maintaining that no one is "able to hurt one who is vigilant and sober in the Lord," while exhorting his reader to endure all painful things bravely that we may obtain those everlasting and pure blessings in Christ Jesus our Lord, to whom be glory and power, now and ever throughout all ages. Amen."

The peace of God will fill our minds, hearts, and souls when we decide to free ourselves from the fear of what men can do to us. To have peace, we must lose all fear. We need to make the decision that we will continue glorifying God no matter what happens to us, because our faith is based on the greatness of Jesus Christ, not on what God does for us. We need to learn to trust Jesus who walks with us every step of the way in this life. We will not have peace and be happy, until we put ourselves and those we love in the hands of the Lord, and live with Him in the present moment, free from negative thoughts that destroy joy in our hearts. We shall fear nothing, because He is with us. We will not fear criticism or rejection. Illness will hold no terrors for us. We will not fear aging or old age. We will not fear death, because Jesus has conquered death. We will not fear the lack of money or anything that might happen to us. We will have peace in the name of Jesus. We are happy in the name of the Lord who gives us strength for every necessity. No one can rob us of His peace, nor make us unhappy, because we belong to Him.

Furthermore, we have to make a definite decision that we will not suffer because of unfulfilled desires and expectations, by detaching ourselves from them. We need to renounce our desires and expectations and receive the joy of the Lord into our souls. In Christ, we can give up suffering, thanking Him for the strength, health, and love that He gives us with His Body and Blood in the Eucharist and His Word that make it possible for us to live detached from desires and the dependencies they create and our own expectations.

The masters of the spiritual life have always taught the necessity of purifying our wills by the practice of self-denial and detachment. According to Garrigou-Lagrange, "The fruit of the purification of the will...is peace, the tranquility of order in which the soul is established with respect to God and to neighbor" (*Three Ages* I: 376).

Our culture has programmed our minds to have many false attitudes that cause us to suffer. Our wishes to follow the trends of the culture have created in us dependencies that make us unhappy and rob us of our peace. We just have to have the latest thing we see advertised on television and feel that our happiness depends on our having it. We have many unrealistic expectations about what our lives should be, and when we cannot attain to them, we agonize and suffer. So what is the solution? We have to deprogram our minds, so that we live in the pure light of the Word of God.

We must learn who we are in Christ and be set free from our desires, dependencies, and expectations. God made us in his own image and likeness. What does this mean? How are we like God? Perhaps a better question might be: How can we become like God? St. John in his first epistle gives us insights to help us understand. He writes: "Dearly beloved, we are now the sons of God, and it has not yet appeared what we shall be. We know that, when He shall appear, we shall be like to Him, because we shall see Him as he is" (I Jn 3:2). He also says: "And every man that has this hope in him purifies himself, even as He is pure" (I Jn 3:3). Most importantly, St. John tells us: "God is love."

If we want to be like God, we too must be love. In a mighty act of His outpouring love, He brought the world into being, and God created us. Our parents conceived us in love. Love is our destiny—love is our life. As God is love, we, also, are love, or are becoming love. Jesus tells us that He is the way, the truth and the life. Therefore God is also truth, and if we want to be like Him, we must be truth. The more we become love and truth, the greater our happiness will be. We were created for love, truth, and happiness—and the peace of God. We need to repeat to ourselves daily: "I am love, I am truth, I am happiness." If we do this daily, in this life, we shall become like Him, so that we will be able to see him as He is, when we come into the light of the brightness of eternity and behold Him face to face.

Let us live the truth day by day, by accepting our lives without illusions, unsatisfied desires, and unrealistic expectations, and by being happy at the present moment, as we rid ourselves of all negativity, and by not depending on anyone or anything for our happiness. No person can give us lasting happiness; only God can give us happiness. No one can take away our peace, for the God of peace, happiness, and joy dwells in our souls. When we live in union with Him, we are love—we are happiness. We live one day at time, free of desires, expectations, and all negativity. The only thing we have to do to be happy is be happy.

We are like trees planted near water that flourish and bloom. The water that gives us life is the Word of God and the presence of Jesus Christ. We draw water from the doctrine and teaching of the Savior and from our union with Him. If we sin, we suffer, and life becomes an agony when we are lost in great sin. Sin is slavery and people who are free do not need to sin. St. John explains: "Whosoever abides in him sins not; whosoever sins has not seen him, neither known him" (I Jn 3:6). When we are free, we embrace the truth Christ came to give us, for He Himself is Truth. We must be ourselves in order to find peace. We do not want just the appearances of truth, but Truth itself. As we come to understand Christ who is the Truth, we realize that He has a plan for our lives—a plan of joy and happiness and spiritual abundance. When we embrace His plan, we can live in peace, reconciled with Him and with everyone else.

"Lord we know that you love us just the way we are, but to draw closer to you and to avoid the suffering that comes from our desires, dependencies, and our expectations, we put our lives in Your Hands. We renounce all sin, for it too brings suffering. Teach us to live lives free of suffering in the light of Your truth and love. We renounce the programming that our culture has given us that is in opposition to the pure truths of Your gospel. We shun the ways of the world, the flesh, and the devil, and open our spirits to receiving Your wisdom and direction for our lives. Teach us to love the way You love—to love the Heavenly Father and the Holy Spirit with Your love. Teach us to love others as You have loved us. May love become perfect in us, casting out all fear, so that only love remains.

"Heavenly Father, we glorify You and thank You that You sent us Jesus to teach us how to love. Holy Spirit, you are the very love that unites the Father and the Son and makes us one with Them. Fill us with your love so that we may truly enter into the life of the Blessed Trinity that will be our home forever. Come, Holy Spirit, and fill us with your gifts and fruits that we may adore the Holy and Immortal Trinity in spirit and in truth with a love that will ever grow stronger and purer. Amen."

14

Praise Brings Peace

If we really desire to possess our souls in peace, we will praise God, for praise always gives us peace and makes us grow in love, and love, in turn, brings even more peace to our minds and hearts. What does it mean to praise God? What does the Word of God tell us about praise?

Let's consider the Holy Scripture. When Leah gave birth to her fourth son of Jacob at Paddan-aram, she named him Juda or Yehudah and said, "Now I will praise the Lord!" (Ge 29:35). The name Juda means praise and the descendants of this son of Jacob and Leah formed the tribe of Judah, and they became people of praise. Most significantly, Jesus was a descendant of this son of Leah. Known as a people of praise, Jews take their name from Judah, and every righteous Jew praises God many times a day.

The first description in Holy Scripture of the children of Israel praising God occurred after the miraculous destruction of Pharaoh's army, as it pursued the children of Israel into the Red Sea, hoping to defeat them totally. Overjoyed that the Lord had delivered them from Egypt and the military might that sought to destroy them, the Israelites sang a canticle to the Lord:

> Let us sing to the Lord: for He is gloriously magnified—the horse and the rider He has thrown into the sea.
> The Lord is my strength and my praise, and he is become salvation to me.
> He is my God and I will glorify Him—the God of my father—and I will exalt Him.
> The Lord is as a man of war. Almighty is His name.
> (Ex 15: 1–3)

Singing of how Pharoah's chariots and his army were cast into the sea, they tell of how they sank like a stone into the depths of the waters.

The waters were gathered together, the floods stood upright as a heap, and the depths were congealed in the heart of the sea.

And with the blast of Your anger, the waters were gathered together. The flowing water stood, the depths were gathered together in the midst of the sea.

Your wind blew and the sea covered them. They sank as lead in the mighty waters.

Who is like to You, among the strong, O Lord? Who is like to You, glorious in holiness, terrible and praiseworthy, doing wonders? You stretched forth your hand, and the earth swallowed them.

In Your mercy, You have been a leader to the people, which you have redeemed, and in Your strength, you have carried them to Your holy habitation.

Let fear and dread fall upon them, in the greatness of Your arm. Let them become unmovable as a stone, until Your people, O Lord, pass by—until this Your people pass by, which You have possessed.

You shall bring them in, and plant them in the mountain of Your inheritance, in Your most firm habitation, which You have made, O Lord—Your sanctuary, O Lord, which Your hands have established. The Lord shall reign for ever and ever.

For Pharaoh went in on horseback with his chariots and horsemen into the sea, and the Lord brought back upon them the waters of the sea, but the children of Israel walked on dry ground in the midst thereof.

As they praised God for His deliverance, singing, "The Lord shall reign forever and ever." Miriam, the prophetess, danced with many women, with timbrels in hand, as they cried out: "Sing to the Lord, for He has triumphed gloriously; the horse and his rider has He thrown into the sea." (Ex 15)

In this hymn of praise, God's people pour forth all the thoughts of their hearts to Him, praising Him for the marvelous rescue and escape from the evil forces of the Egyptians. Significantly, they joined dancing and music to their praise.

In the book of Leviticus, we read that Moses asked Aaron to make offerings to God for sin at the altar, telling him: "Do it and His glory will appear to you." (Le 9:6–93). Aaron did as he was told, blessing the people and offering a holocaust for their sins. Together Moses and Aaron entered the tabernacle of testimony, and then came out and blessed the people. As the holocaust was consumed, the glory of the Lord appeared to them all, and they fell on their faces and praised the Lord (9:23). We are not told the words of their praise, but we can imagine that each one individually praised God in the depths of his soul for the glory of the Lord that had been revealed to them.

On another occasion Moses addressed his people and told them that they must fear the Lord, walk in His ways, and love Him, and serve Him with all their heart and soul (De 10:12). They are to keep His commandments and observe His ceremonies, circumcising their hearts (10:16). Moses said: "He is your praise, and Your God that has done for you these great and terrible things, which your eyes have seen" (10:21).

Then Moses explained to the people: "And the Lord has chosen you this day, to be His peculiar people—as He has spoken to you—and to keep all His commandments, and to make you higher than all nations which he Has created, to His own praise, and name, and glory, that you may be a holy people of the Lord your God, as He has spoken" (De 26:18–19). Here the word "peculiar" mean unique—God's people are to be distinct from all others. Having been created to be a people of praise that they may be holy, God has entered into a covenant with them. How much more should we be a people of praise, since God sent His son to redeem us and by His death and resurrection to enter into a greater covenant with us than He did with the ancient Hebrew people. Nevertheless, we can learn much about praising God from His saints of old, such as King David.

King David was a man who knew how to praise God. Praise was ever on his lips and in his heart. It is not enough to form words of praise with our mouths; our hearts must be filled with praise. Consider how David praised God, when he was delivered from his enemy Saul. With utter and complete trust in God he proclaims:

> The Lord is my rock, and my strength, and my savior. God is my strong one, in Him will I trust—my shield, and the horn of my salvation.
>
> He lifts me up, and is my refuge! My Savior, You will deliver me from iniquity. I will call on the Lord who is worthy to be praised. I shall be saved from my enemies, for the pangs of death have surrounded me.
>
> The floods of Belial have made me afraid. The cords of hell compassed me. The snares of death prevented me.
>
> In my distress, I will call upon the Lord. I will cry to my God, and He will hear my voice out of his temple, and my cry shall come to His ears.
>
> The earth shook and trembled, the foundations of the mountains were moved, and shaken, because He was angry with them.
>
> A smoke went up from His nostrils, and a devouring fire out of His mouth—coals were kindled by it.
>
> He bowed the heavens, and came down, and darkness was under His feet. And He rode upon the cherubim, and flew, and slid upon the wings of the wind.
>
> He made darkness a covering round about him, dropping waters out of the clouds of the heavens. By the brightness before him, the coals of fire were kindled.
>
> The Lord shall thunder from heaven. The Most High shall give forth His voice.

He shot arrows and scattered them—lightning—and consumed them. And the overflowing of the sea appeared.

The foundations of the world were laid open at the rebuke of the Lord, at the blast of the Spirit of his wrath.

He sent from on high, and took me, and drew me out of many waters. He delivered me from my most mighty enemy, and from them that hated me, for they were too strong for me.

David continues his prayer, by recalling the wondrous deeds of God. His heart is overflowing with praise as he sings:

For You are my lamp, O Lord: and You, O Lord, will enlighten my darkness. For in thee, I will run girded—in my God I will leap over the wall.

God—His way is immaculate—the word of the Lord is tried by fire; He is the shield of all that trust in him.

Who is God, but the Lord, and who is strong, but our God? God who has girded me with strength, and made my way perfect.

Continuing his prayer, David tells what he is going to do with the help of the Lord. He concludes with more praise:

The Lord lives, and my God is blessed, and the strong God of my salvation shall be exalted—God who gives me revenge, and brings down people under me, Who brings me forth from my enemies, and lifts me up from them that resist me.

From the wicked man, You shall deliver me. Therefore will I give thanks to You, O Lord, among the Gentiles, and will sing to Your name—giving great salvation to his king, and showing mercy to David His anointed, and to his seed forever. (II Sam 22: 1–51)

We can make David's prayer our own, for the Lord has delivered us all from the enemies of our souls and blessed us. There is no more beautiful way to praise God than with His holy Word. David's prayer requires an explanation when he says that the snares of death prevented him." Prevent is a very old English word coming from the Latin *praevenire*—to come before. In other words, David is saying that the snares of death rose up before him.

When David put the ark of the covenant containing the tablets with the Ten Commandments in a tent and appointed Levites—priests—to minister, glorify, and praise the Lord with psalms, harps, and cymbals, two priests Banaias and Jaziel continually sounded trumpets before the ark of God. Here is how they praised God: "Praise ye the Lord, and call upon His name. Make known His doings among the nations. Sing to Him, yea, sing praises to Him, and relate all his wondrous works (I Ch 16: 8–9).

> Praise ye His holy name! Let the heart of them rejoice, that seek the Lord! Seek ye the Lord, and His power! Seek ye his face evermore!
>
> Let all the earth be moved at His presence, for He has founded the world immoveable. Let the heavens rejoice, and the earth be glad, and let them say among the nations: "The Lord has reigned."
>
> Let the sea roar, and the fullness thereof. Let the fields rejoice, and all things that are in them. Then shall the trees of the wood give praise before the Lord, because He is come to judge the earth.
>
> Give ye glory to the Lord, for He is good, for His mercy endures for ever! And say: "Save us, O God our Savior, and gather us together, and deliver us from the nations, that we may give glory to Your holy name, and may rejoice in singing your praises."
>
> Blessed be the Lord the God of Israel from eternity to eternity! And let all the people say "Amen," and a hymn to God. (I Ch 16: 30–36)

A glorious example of the praise of God is recounted when the priests bring the ark of the covenant into the temple that Solomon built, placing it in the holy of holies under the wings of the cherubim (II Ch 5:7). The Levites and the cantors were all dressed in fine linen. They sounded their cymbals, played their harps, together with a hundred and twenty priests sounding trumpets (2 Ch 5:12). The sound of the trumpets, the voices, cymbals, organs, and various other kinds of musical instruments were so loud that they could be heard from quite a distance. When they began praising the Lord, recalling that His mercy endures forever, the temple was filled with a cloud.

God inhabits the praises of His people. Here we find a very powerful example of this. There is no doubt that some kind of theophany took place at this awesome celebration. When the Scripture says that the house of God was filled with a cloud, this recalls the cloud that the Lord used to guide His people through the desert into the Promised Land. The cloud is a symbol of the presence of God. We also recall that when Jesus ascended from the Mount of Olives, he was taken up into a cloud. In this ceremony in Solomon's temple with the ark, the presence of God was so powerful that the priests were unable to minister, for the glory of the Lord filled His house. Let this be an inspiration to us to praise Him who is worthy of all praise.

Awed at the majesty of God, Solomon exclaimed "Is it credible then that God should dwell with men on the earth? If heaven and the heavens of heavens do not contain You, how much less this house, which I have built?" (II Ch 6:18).

Imploring the Lord, he said, "For You are my God. Let your eyes, I beseech You, be open, and let Your ears be attentive to the prayer, that is made in this place" (II Ch 6:40).

When Solomon finished praying, fire came down from heaven and consumed the holocausts and the victims, and the majesty of the Lord filled the house (II Ch 7:1). Because the glory of the Lord filled the temple, the priests could not enter it. When the children of Israel saw the fire consume the holocaust and the glory and majesty of the Lord, they fell down with their faces on the stone pavement and adored and praised the Lord, because He is good and His mercy endures forever (II Ch 7:2–3).

If we want to praise God, surely no better way can be found than to use the book of Psalms as our prayer book. It is the prayer book that Jesus and the apostles used at the Last Supper. As He was dying on the cross, quoting from the twenty-first psalm, He said, "My God, my God, why have You forsaken me?" The book of Psalms is *the* prayer book of the Church.

The psalms are filled with joy and peace. The psalmist sings: "Blessed are they that dwell in Your house, O Lord: they shall praise You forever and ever" (83:5). "Come let us praise the Lord with joy; let us joyfully sing to God our Savior" (94:1). "Seven times a day I have given praise to You, for the judgments of your justice" (118:16). "Every day I will bless you, and I will praise Your name forever—yes, forever and ever" (144:2).

In a mighty burst of fervor, the psalmist calls on all creatures, great and small, to praise the Lord. "Praise Him, all His angels! Praise Him, all His hosts. Praise ye Him, O sun and moon! Praise Him, all ye stars and light!" (148:2–3). Even the dragons and the deeps are invited to praise God (128:7). Fire, hail, snow, ice, and stormy winds, mountains, and hills, trees, beasts, cattle, and even serpents and feathered fowls are asked to join in the praise of God. Kings and princes, young and old all are invited to join in the psalmist's glorious hymn of praise.

Just like the people of the Bible, we are called to be a people of praise who sing the glory of His grace. Praise is not just repeating, "Praise the Lord!" because others are saying it. Praise must come from the heart. If it is not heartfelt it is worthless. We need to be like the little boy who was watching a thunderstorm from his bedroom window. When a great streak of lightning came crashing through the night sky, the child yelled, "Do it again, Lord!"

We need to drink in the majesty of our world with its glorious mountain peaks and verdant valleys, and let our hearts rise up in gratitude to the One who made it. All we need to do is breathe a simple prayer. "It's beautiful, Lord!" Praise is easy when we just consider all that the Lord has done for us. We should praise

Him a hundred times each day, praising Him for all the wonderful things that surround us in our daily lives. We should especially praise Him for His grace that redeems and sanctifies us.

In the biblical accounts of praise, we noted that the praise of the people could be heard from quite a distance. When we praise God in our churches, we should do it with enthusiasm and verve. Nothing is worse than a dead church where no one sings and praises God like they really mean it. Nothing is more beautiful than a congregation that sings the praise of God joyfully and triumphantly, lifting holy hands in prayer, as St. Paul advises (I Tm 2:8).

We need to put enthusiasm in our praise. According to Isaiah, all nature rejoices in the praise of God: "You shall go out with joy, and be led forth with peace. The mountains and the hills shall sing praise before You, and all the trees of the country shall clap their hands" (Is 55:12).

Let us sing "Alleluia!" joyfully to God. When we do, we are linked to the ancient tradition of the people of the Bible who interspersed their prayers and praise by chanting it. The word "alleluia" comes from the Hebrew words *hallel*, meaning praise, and Yah, an abbreviated form of Yahweh, the Hebrew name for God. When we say "Alleluia," we are saying "Praise God!" Like the people of the Bible, we can also add dance to our praise. David danced before the ark of God and rejoiced. Can we do anything less? We who have so much more to praise Him for, since He has redeemed us with His blood.

St. Paul tells us that we should be filled with the Holy Spirit, rejoicing in psalms, and hymns, and spiritual canticles, singing and making melody in our hearts to the Lord (Ep 5: 18–19). The psalmist tells us to sing unto the Lord a new song. We can actually compose a song in our own words to praise Him. If words fail us, we can ask Him for the gift of tongues, so that we can praise Him in the Spirit.

In our approach to praise, we need to be creative, and let the Spirit inspire us how to praise the Holy and Immortal Trinity. When we do not know how to praise the Triune God, the Spirit Himself will pray in us and direct our prayer and make it pleasing to God.

"Come, Holy Spirit, teach us how to perfect our praise. Fill us with Your presence and pray in us and with us. Flood our souls with Your peace that passes all understanding. Inspire us with love that our hearts may rise up to You and dwell in You forever. Praise to the Most Holy Trinity! We give you all the honor, glory, and praise, now and forever. Amen."

15

The Sacrament of Peace

On the night He was betrayed, the Lord Jesus took bread, and after He had given thanks, broke it and gave it to His disciples, saying: "Take, eat, this is My Body. And after He had supped, He took the chalice and said "This chalice is the new testament in My blood…" (I Co 11:24–35). Since the Lord Himself tells us that in the great mystery of the altar, He is giving us His Body and Blood to become our very life, who could dare to doubt Him? The Church has always believed and taught that Jesus is truly present in this wondrous sacrament. Let us consider what the Church has told us about this great mystery of our faith from the earliest times.

One of the oldest Christian writings still extant is the *Didache,* which is also known as *The Teaching of the Twelve Apostles.* Some scholars maintain that this work was written as early as the year 50, others place it around 80 to 90, and a few others, a little later. According to the *Didache,* Christians are to gather together on Sunday, the Lord's day, and break bread and give thanks, after first having confessed their sins so that their "sacrifice may be pure" (14:1). If anyone had a quarrel with anyone, s/he was not permitted to join the assembly until they were reconciled, so that the sacrifice would "not be defiled" (14:2). We must note here that the Eucharist was regarded in the *Didache* as a sacrifice and identified with the sacrifice of Malachi 14:11: "For from the rising of the sun even to the going down, My Name is great among the Gentiles, and in every place there is sacrifice, and there is offered to My Name a clean oblation, for My Name is great among the Gentiles, says the Lord of Hosts" (14:3). The sacrifice of the Holy Eucharist has been offered daily ever since, even to the ends of the earth.

St. Ignatius of Antioch, considered one of the Apostolic Fathers, because, together with his friend Polycarp, he heard St. John the Evangelist preach, gives us some penetrating insights into the mystery of the Eucharist. Born in Syria around the year 50, St. Ignatius received his episcopal consecration from the hands of the apostles and was appointed by the Apostle Peter as the third bishop of Antioch, the next largest city of the empire after Rome, and the place where followers of Jesus were first called Christians. He succeeded St. Evodius who was the immediate successor of St. Peter in the see of Antioch. During the persecution of Domitian, Ignatius longed for martyrdom, but was glad when peace was restored, for he feared that some of his people might have been too weak to endure martyrdom. When the persecution of Trajan was underway, he appeared before the emperor in the year 98 and confessed his faith in Christ. He even told Trajan that his name was Theophorus, meaning the God bearer, because, as He explained to the emperor, he carried Christ within his breast. When Trajan asked him if he carried within himself the One who was crucified, he replied "Truly so, for it is written, 'I will dwell in them, and walk in them'" (*Martyrdom* Ch II).

Hearing this, Emperor Trajan passed the death sentence on him, commanding the one who claimed he bore within himself the Crucified to be bound and taken to Rome to be devoured by wild beasts. When he heard this, Ignatius was overjoyed and cried out: "Thank You, O Lord, that You have vouchsafed to honor me with a perfect love towards You and have made me be bound with iron chains, like Your Apostle Paul."

The account of the martyrdom of Ignatius, reputed to have been written by one Philo, deacon of Tarsus and one Rheus Agathopus, a Syrian, recounts how these two set men out with him from Syria, stopping at Smyrna where he visited Polycarp, with whom he had been a disciple of the Apostle John. At Smyrna, where Ignatius stayed for a lengthy time, representatives from various communities of Christians in Asia Minor came to see him. Ephesus, Magnesia, and Tralles sent groups to comfort him. In turn, he wrote letters to these churches and a letter to Rome. In fact, he wrote a series of letters—we have seven of them—to the various churches. It is from these letters that we learn of the teaching about the Eucharist that he received from the apostles.

Upon leaving Smyrna, the soldiers guarding him took him to Troas, and from there, he wrote letters to the churches of Philadelphia and Smyrna and one to Polycarp. From Troas, they sailed to Neapolis, and then traveled overland through Macedonia and Illyria. Finally reaching Epirus, they found a ship and sailed the Adriatic and thence into the Tyrrhene until they came to Puteoli, where Ignatius wished to disembark, because he wanted to follow in the footsteps of St. Paul from there to Rome. Because of violent wind, he was unable to do this, and the ship sailed on to the harbor of Rome. Ignatius expressed his haste to get to Rome, so he could quickly go to the Lord he loved. The journey from Syria to Rome lasted nine years. At every stop along the way massive groups of Christians came to greet him.

Upon his arrival in Rome, he learned that some people there were going to try to save him from death, and he begged them not to, so eager was he to receive the palm of martyrdom. Although it was almost the end of the day when they arrived, there were large crowds gathered to see the spectacle of wild animals devouring Christians, because it was a special day. It was on the twentieth of December, in the year 107 that Ignatius of Antioch was thrown to the lions in the Roman Coliseum. They devoured him almost completely, with the few bones that remained, lovingly gathered by the Christians, who wrapped them in linen, giving them to Philo of Celicia and Rheus Agathopus to carry them back to the church in Antioch.

Let us now see what St. Ignatius, a disciple of St. John the Evangelist, has to say to us about the Eucharist as, in a letter, he beseeches the Romans not to try to prevent his martyrdom.

> Suffer me to become food for the wild beasts, through whose instrumentality, it will be granted me to attain to God. I am the wheat of God, and am ground by the teeth of the wild beasts, that I may be found the pure bread of God. Rather entice the wild beasts that they may become my tomb, and may leave nothing of my body; so that when I am dead, I may not be found troublesome to anyone. Then shall I be a true disciple of Jesus Christ, when the world shall not see so much as my body. Entreat the Lord for me, that by these instruments I may be found a sacrifice to God. (4)

After pleading with the Romans not to intervene and try to prevent his martyrdom, he speaks of the Body and Blood of Christ.

> For though I am alive while I write to you, yet I am eager to die. My love has been crucified, and there is no fire in me desiring to be fed; but there is within me a water that lives and speaks, saying to me inwardly, "Come to the Father." I have no delight in corruptible food, nor in the pleasures of this life. I desire the bread of God, the heavenly bread, the bread of life, which is the flesh of Jesus Christ, the Son of God, who became afterwards of the seed of David and Abraham; and I desire the drink of God, namely His blood, which is incorruptible love and eternal life.

Here St. Ignatius links the Eucharist to everlasting life. When we receive the Body and Blood of Christ we are receiving our life and incorruptible love which will endure forever. Ignatius concludes this letter by asking the people of Rome to pray that he may attain martyrdom for Jesus Christ and to pray for his church at Antioch. In his letter to the Smyrnaeans, he writes more of the Eucharist, as he warns the recipients of his letter against heretics that do not believe in the blood of Christ.

> Let no man deceive himself. Both the things which are in heaven, and the glorious angels, and rulers, both visible and invisible, if they believe not in the blood of Christ, shall, in consequence, incur condemnation" (6)
>
> They abstain from the Eucharist and from prayer, because they confess not the Eucharist to be the flesh of our Savior Jesus Christ, which suffered for our sins, and which the Father, of His goodness, raised up again. Those, therefore, who speak against this gift of God, incur death in the midst of their disputes. But it were better for them to treat it with respect, that they also might rise again.

Here St. Ignatius is echoing the words of Christ that unless we eat His flesh and drink His blood, we will have no life in us. And if we do, He will raise us up on the last day.

In his letter to the Ephesians, S. Ignatius refers to the Eucharist as the "medicine of immortality" and the "antidote to prevent us from dying" that makes us live forever in Christ Jesus (20). This is a strong expression of his belief that the consecrated bread is the Body of Jesus and the consecrated wine, His Blood. No mere symbol could be called the "medicine of immortality." The way this saint went joyfully to his death in the Coliseum, being devoured by lions, confirms his believe in the indwelling presence of Jesus Christ and the reality of His Body and Blood in the Holy Eucharist. Interestingly his writings are the oldest ones extant which refer to the Church as the "Catholic Church."

Another early Christian who suffered martyrdom and wrote inspiring words about the Holy Eucharist was Justin, known to us as St. Justin Martyr. He was born near the beginning of the second century in the land of the Bible at Flavia Neapolis, a town founded by Vespasian in the year 72 AD. It was the ancient Sichem, capital of Samaria, and today is known as Nablus. Although he was a Samaritan by birth, he was of pagan Greek descent and spoke of himself as uncircumcised. His father Priscos and his grandfather Baccheios were sent by Vespasian's son Titus to live in Palestine in a colony he established there.

Hungering for truth, Justin pursued the study of philosophy. He listened as Jewish teachers expounded their ancient faith to him. Having been disappointed with the Stoics, Peripatetics, and Pythagoreans, he took up Platonism in his search for God. In his dialog with Trypho, he wrote: "I expected forthwith to look upon God, for this is the end of Plato's philosophy."

One day, as he was walking near the sea at Ephesus, he encountered a mysterious old man who, noticing that Justin wore the palium of the philosophers, chanced to speak with him about the things of God, pointing out to him that it was impossible for human reason to attain to God. He directed Justin to read the ancient Hebrew prophets and their prophecies concerning the Messiah. He enjoined Justin to pray that light be given him, because the things of God can be perceived only by those to whom Christ gives wisdom. About his encounter with the old man, Justin wrote: "But straightway a flame was kindled in my soul, and a love of the prophets and of those men who are friends of Christ possessed me, and while revolving his words in my mind, I found this philosophy alone to be safe and profitable" (*Trypho* 8). He embraced the Catholic faith about the year 130.

After living for a time at Ephesus, Justin went twice to Rome where he set up a school in his own home, attracting some well-known students such as St. Irenaeus of Lyons and Tatian, among others. He wrote a great deal in defense of the Christian religion and preached Christ to all who would listen. The prefect Rusticus condemned him to death for his faith about the year 165, together with his six companions, because they refused to sacrifice to the Roman gods.

In no uncertain terms, Justin told the emperor that he would not sacrifice to them, saying "No one in his right mind gives up piety for impiety."

When the prefect warned Justin and his companions that if they did not obey and sacrifice to the gods, they would be tortured without mercy, Justin replied, "That is our desire, to be tortured for our Lord Jesus Christ, and so to be saved, for that will give us salvation and firm confidence at the more terrible universal tribunal of Our Lord and Savior." They were all scourged and beheaded, according to the law; they died glorifying God and confessing their faith in Jesus Christ.

Now let us examine what this great man of God has to say about the faith of the early Church in the Eucharist.

> And this food is called among us the Eucharist, of which no one is allowed to partake, but the man who believes that the things which we teach are true, and who has been washed with the washing that is for the remission of sins, and unto regeneration, and who is so living as Christ has enjoined. For not as common bread and common drink do we receive these, but in like manner as Jesus Christ our Savior, having been made flesh by the Word of God, had both flesh and blood for our salvation, so likewise have we been taught that the food which is blessed by the prayer of His word, and from which our blood and flesh by transmutation are nourished, is the flesh and blood of that Jesus who was made flesh. (*First Apology* Ch LXVI)

Obviously St. Justin had a firm faith in the reality of the Eucharist as the Body and Blood of Jesus. In his dialog with Trypho, he also identifies the Eucharist with the sacrifice of Malachi, as did St. Ignatius, and sees it as replacing the temple sacrifices of the ancient Jewish people.

Another writer that hands on to us the teaching of the apostles is St. Irenaeus, Bishop of Lyons and a disciple of St. John the Evangelist, who was martyred February 23, 156 at the age of 86. He saw and heard the preaching of St. Polycarp. St Irenaeus was born in Asia Minor about the year 125. He went to Gaul to minister to the people there who were converting from paganism to the Catholic faith. As a priest of the church of Lyons, he was sent to Rome with a letter to Pope Eleutherius, during the reign of Marcus Aurelius. While he was absent from Lyons, St. Pothinus, his bishop, was martyred for the faith, and upon his return to Gaul, Irenaeus was made Bishop of Lyons. In his writings, he describes the faith as it was practiced at that time. He died near the end of the second century or the beginning of the third. According to Gregory of Tours, he was martyred, but we have no account of his martyrdom. His remains were interred under the altar of the church of St. John in Lyons, which was later named after St. Irenaeus. Unfortunately, his tomb was destroyed by the Calvinists in 1562 and his relics lost.

In his work *Adversus Haereses, Against Heresies*, St. Irenaeus presents the theological and doctrinal teachings of the Catholic Church, as he received them from St. Polycarp. Speaking of the Eucharist, he wrote:

> He [Jesus] has acknowledged the cup...as His own blood, from which He bedews our blood; and the bread...He has established as His own body, from which He gives increase to our bodies.
>
> And just as a cutting from the vine planted in the ground fructifies in its season, or as a corn of wheat falling into the earth and becoming decomposed, rises with manifold increase by the Spirit of God, who contains all things, and then, through the wisdom of God, serves for the use of men, and having received the Word of God, becomes the Eucharist, which is the body and blood of Christ; so also our bodies, being nourished by it, and deposited in the earth, and suffering decomposition there, shall rise at their appointed time, the Word of God granting them resurrection to the glory of God. (5:2:2–3)

Here Irenaeus is telling us just exactly what Jesus said. If we eat His Flesh and drink His Blood we shall have life and He will raise us up on the last day. The Eucharist is the medicine of immortality, because it is truly the Body and Blood of Jesus and contains His soul and divinity. In the Eucharist Jesus gives Himself totally to us in an inexhaustible act of love.

Although Tertullian was never canonized, he is one of the great fathers of the early Church, and the first to write in Latin. He is the one who coined the word "Trinity" to describe the persons of God. He is also famous for saying the blood of the martyrs is the seed of the Church.

Quintus Septimus Florens Terullianus was born in Carthage, present day Tunisia, around 155 to 160, to pagan parents who provided him with a good education in literature, philosophy, rhetoric and law. There is some evidence to support the belief that his father was a centurion in an African legion. Having completed his education in Carthage, Tertullian went to Rome when he was about twenty years old and began his career as a lawyer. While he was in Rome, Tertullian became interested in Christianity and when he returned to Carthage, about the end of the second century, he became a Christian. What influenced him to do so was the heroism of the martyrs, the moral rectitude of Christians, and their belief in God. In Africa, many Christians were martyred during his lifetime, including Perpetua and Felicity, both mentioned in the canon of the Mass, and it is believed that he wrote the account of their martyrdom.

Tertullian became a teacher, instructing those who presented themselves for baptism, and a writer who defended the Christian faith. If St. Jerome is correct, Tertullian was ordained a priest. Most of the details of his life are found in biographies written by people like Jerome and Eusebius who lived much later in time than Tertullian. Some details of his life can be perceived from his writings.

Around the year 210 or perhaps a little earlier, Tertullian joined a sect known as Montanism, named after one Montanus who claimed that the Holy Spirit was giving new revelations to the Church. The sect was referred to as New Prophecy, practiced severe asceticism, and anticipated that Christ would return soon. Tertullian embraced Montanism, according to Jerome, because he was distressed over the envy and laxity of the Roman clergy. He became a spokesman for Montanism, which was later condemned by the pope, until he decided that the Montanists were not rigorous enough for him, and he founded his own sect, the Tertullians, which existed in Africa until the fifth century. However, we must point out that his statements about the Eucharist are quiet orthodox and have nothing of the Montanists or Tertullians about them. Tertullian died about 230, the date of his last writings.

In his work *On the Resurrection of the Flesh*, he writes the following about how Christians are fattened on God by partaking of the Holy Eucharist.

> It would suffice to say, indeed, that there is not a soul that can at all procure salvation, except it believe whilst it is in the flesh, so true is it that the flesh is

the very condition on which salvation hinges. And since the soul is, in consequence of its salvation, chosen to the service of God, it is the flesh which actually renders it capable of such service. The flesh, indeed, is washed, in order that the soul may be cleansed; the flesh is anointed, that the soul may be consecrated; the flesh is signed (with the cross), that the soul too may be fortified; the flesh is shadowed with the imposition of hands, that the soul also maybe illuminated by the Spirit; the flesh feeds on the body and blood of Christ, that the soul likewise may fatten on *its* God. (8).

Another great theologian and Father of the Church was Origen or Origenes Adamantius, who was born to Christian parents in Alexandria. His father Leonides, who gave him his first years of education, teaching him the Bible, was martyred when persecution of Christians took place during the rule of Septimus Severus. Origen, longed for martyrdom, and would have followed his father to his death, except his mother prevented it, by taking all his clothes and hiding them, leaving him completely naked in his room.

Upon the death of his father, Origen took on the responsibility of caring for many little brothers and sisters and his mother. With the education his father had given him, he reopened the catechetical school at Alexandria, which had been run by St. Clement, before the persecution. He raised a little money by selling his library for an income of about twelve pieces of silver a day. He taught during the day and devoted himself to study at night.

One of the strange things that happened during his life occurred when, it is reported, that he castrated himself, supposedly to avoid any suggestion of scandal, when he was entrusted with the teaching of women. Under Roman law this was a capital crime.

During the reign of Emperor Caracalla, about 211 or 212, Origen visited Rome, but was disillusioned by the laxity he saw there while Zephyrinus was pope. When he returned to Alexandria, because of the large numbers of those wanting to enter the Church, he had to employ one Heraclas to teach the catechumens. About 213 or 214, Origen visited Arabia and spent some time in the rose city of Petra. Although he was not as yet ordained, he was invited to preach in Jerusalem and vicinity. After he returned to Egypt, Caracalla's soldiers plundered Alexandria and closed the schools, causing Origen to leave and go to Casearea, only to return to Alexandria in 216.

About the year 230, he visited Caesarea again, and the church there ordained him, so that Demetrius, his bishop, would have no reason to complain of his preaching. Feeling that his rights were infringed upon, Demetrius held two synods, which banished Origen from Alexandria and declared his ordination to be invalid. Henceforth Origen made his home at Caesarea, where he continued teaching dialectics, physics, ethics, and metaphysics. He also continued his research and his writing and dedicated himself to preaching.

In the persecution of 240, he was arrested, tortured, and bound hand and foot to a block. Although he did not yield to the torture, it resulted in his death. (Jerome 54: 13)

Now let us consider his comments on the Holy Eucharist.

> We give thanks to the Creator of all, and, along with thanksgiving and prayer for the blessings we have received, we also eat the bread presented to us; and this bread becomes by prayer a sacred body, which sanctifies those who sincerely partake of it. (*Against Celsus* 8:33)

In his Homilies on Numbers, he speak further of the Eucharist.

> ...now, however, in full view, there is the true food, the flesh of the Word of God, as He Himself says: "My flesh is truly food, and my blood is truly drink." (7:2)

After the prayer of epiclesis, the elements of bread and wine are changed into the Body and Blood of Jesus. So the Church has continued to teach down through the centuries.

Some of the clearest and most beautiful teaching of the early Church on the Eucharist can be found in the writings of St. Cyril of Jerusalem, a Doctor of the Church. Born in 317, Cyril was reared in the church of Jerusalem. Ordained a priest about 346, he was put in charge of delivering catechetical lectures to the catechumens by his bishop, St. Maximus. Upon the bishop's death, Cyril was elevated to the episcopacy and became Bishop of Jerusalem in the year 350. Because the church in Jerusalem endured great difficulties due to problems with Arians, Jews, and Manicheans, Cyril had to go into exile a number of times.

On May 7, 351 at nine o'clock in the morning, an extraordinary sign appeared in the Jerusalem sky—a large cross that was as bright as the sun and reached from Golgotha to the Mount of Olives. The apparition continued for several hours, causing many people to convert to Christianity. Cyril even wrote a letter to the emperor about it. The Orthodox Church still celebrates this event every May 7.

When he returned from an exile in 360, he witnessed the attempts by the Emperor Julian the Apostate to rebuild the Temple of Jerusalem in order to prove that Christ's prophecies of Matthew 24:2 were wrong, which are as follows:

"Do you see all these things? Amen I say to you there shall not be left here a stone upon a stone that shall not be destroyed." Citing the prophecy of Daniel 9:26–17, Cyril preached that Julian's attempts to rebuild the temple were sheer vanity. Daniel's prophecy says:

> And after sixty-two weeks Christ shall be slain: and the people that shall deny him shall not be his. And a people with their leader that shall come, shall destroy the city and the sanctuary, and the end thereof shall be waste, and after the end of the war the appointed desolation. (Dn 9:26–27)

Julian's undertaking was doomed to failure. Cyril watched as fire came from the foundations of the temple and the stones that remained overturned, killing many of Julian's workmen.

When famine struck the people of Jerusalem, Cyril sold some things that belonged to the church to provide food for the starving. His enemies picked up on this, and there were rumors that some of the church vestments wound up as clothing for actors. One of his most fierce enemies Acacius, the Arian Bishop of Caesarea, accused him to the emperor with the story that Cyril had sold an expensive gift that the emperor had given the church and that a dancer received it and died wearing it. Consequently, Cyril was banished from Jerusalem. He was returned to his see, when Julian became emperor, but was banished again when Julian's consul reversed the decision. When he was finally permitted to return to Jerusalem eleven years later, the church there was torn by heresy and strife. He attended the Council of Constantinople in 381, when the Nicene Creed and orthodoxy triumphed, and Arianism was finally condemned. This council gave him the justice that was due him and cleared him of all the rumors and even commended him for fighting the Arians. Finally, after eight years of peace in Jerusalem, he died in 386, when he was about seventy years old.

Let us now turn to his twenty-second catechetical lecture on the Eucharist. The lectures were given extemporaneously and some member of the congregation wrote them down as he delivered them. They give us an excellent record of the Catholic faith, as it was believed in the early Church. Cyril begins by recalling St. Paul's comments on the Eucharist (I Co 11:23). He adds that since our Lord himself said that it is His Body and Blood how could we doubt Him.

> Wherefore with full assurance let us partake as of the Body and Blood of Christ, for in the figure of Bread is given to you His Body, and in the figure of Wine His Blood that you by partaking of the Body and Blood of Christ, may be made of the same body and the same blood with Him. For thus we come to

bear Christ in us, because His Body and Blood are distributed through our members; thus it is that, according to the blessed Peter, we became partakers of the divine nature. (3)

St. Cyril believed and taught that the consecrated bread and the consecrated wine become the true body and blood of Christ and that they convey divine life to the one who receives them. He continues:

Consider therefore the Bread and the Wine not as bare elements, for they are, according to the Lord's declaration, the Body and Blood of Christ; for even though sense suggests this to you, yet let faith establish you. Judge not the matter from the taste, but from faith—be fully assured without misgiving, that the Body and Blood of Christ have been given to you. (6)

After assuring his new Christians that they truly receive the Body and Blood of Jesus Christ, he continues:

Having learned these things, and been fully assured that the seeming bread is not bread, though sensible to taste, but the Body of Christ; and that the seeming wine is not wine, though the taste will have it so, but the Blood of Christ; and that of this David sung of old, saying: And bread strengthens man's heart, to makes his face to shine with oil, "strengthen your heart," by partaking thereof as spiritual, and "make the face of your soul to shine." And so having it unveiled with a pure conscience, you may reflect as a mirror the glory of the Lord, and proceed from glory to glory, in Christ Jesus our Lord—to whom be honor, and might, and glory, for ever and ever. Amen. (9)

This is the faith of the Church, in ancient times, and still today. Christ gives Himself—Body and Blood, Soul and Divinity—in the Eucharist to strengthen us so that we may reflect the glory of the Lord.

In his lecture on the sacred liturgy and communion, Cyril identifies the Eucharist with the daily bread that we pray for in the Lord's Prayer (15). As he describes the liturgy we are amazed at how much it resembles our liturgy today. In describing the kiss of peace, he has these words to say concerning our unity in Christ:

Then the Deacon cries aloud, "Receive ye one another; and let us kiss one another." Think not that this kiss is of the same character with those given in public by common friends. It is not such, but this kiss blends souls one with another, and courts entire forgiveness for them. The kiss therefore is the sign that our souls are mingled together, and banishes all remembrance of all wrongs. (3)

Finally in describing the liturgy, Cyril comes to the invitation for the faithful to come forth to receive the Body and Blood of Christ. In this passage we can see how greatly he treasured the Eucharist.

> In approaching therefore, come not with your wrists extended, or your fingers spread; but make your left hand a throne for the right, as for that which is to receive a King. And having hollowed your palm, receive the Body of Christ, saying over it, "Amen." So then after having carefully hallowed your eyes by the touch of the Holy Body, partake of it; giving heed lest you lose any portion thereof; for whatever you lose, is evidently a loss to you as it were from one of your own members. For tell me, if any one gave you grains of gold, would you not hold them with all carefulness, being on your guard against losing any of them, and suffering loss? Will you not then much more carefully keep watch, that not a crumb fall from you of what is more precious than gold and precious stones? (21)

While there are many more beautiful passages that we could quote from the writings of St. Cyril of Jerusalem, there are so many of the Fathers of the early Church who spoke eloquently of the presence of the Lord in the Eucharist that we will continue by now considering what St. Hilary of Poitiers, Bishop and Doctor of the Church had to say about it. Born in Poitiers, in what is today France, to a very illustrious family of Gaul, St. Hilary, although reared a pagan, desired to know about God. With his great love for truth, he realized that polytheism was absurd with its multiple gods, and decided that monotheism was the correct belief. This led him to the Holy Scriptures in which he learned about Moses and how God revealed Himself to him, saying "I am that am." He was further impressed with the first chapter of St. John's gospel about how in the beginning was the Word and the Word became flesh and dwelt among us. Having received the gift of faith, he asked for the Church to baptize him.

Prior to his conversion to the Catholic faith, Hilary married and fathered a daughter. His wife was still living, when he was raised to the episcopacy and consecrated Bishop of Poitiers about the year 353. From the time of his ordination, he lived in continency. Emperor Julian the Apostate banished him in 356, and he remained for three years in exile. It was during this period of time that he wrote *De Trinitate,* which we cite here as to his teaching on the Eucharist. With the death of Emperor Constantius, the Arian persecution ended, and he returned to Poitiers where he died in 368. Although he thirsted for martyrdom, he died a natural death. His relics were eventually taken to St. Denys near Paris. Many miracles have been attributed to his intercession.

Here is how St. Hilary affirms his belief in the Holy Eucharist as the Body and Blood of Jesus Christ.

> Let us read what is written, let us understand what we read, and then fulfill the demands of a perfect faith. For as to what we say concerning the reality of Christ's nature within us, unless we have been taught by Him, our words are foolish and impious. For He says Himself, "My flesh is meat indeed, and My blood is drink indeed. He that eats My flesh and drinks My blood abides in Me, and I in him." As to the verity of the flesh and blood there is no room left for doubt. For now, both from the declaration of the Lord Himself and our own faith, it is verily flesh and verily blood. And these when eaten and drunk, bring it to pass that both we are in Christ and Christ in us. (8:14)

Next, to learn more about the teaching of the early Church concerning the Eucharist, we turn to St. Gregory of Nyssa, also a bishop and one of the Cappadocian Fathers. He was born in the first part of the fourth century in Asia Minor to a very devout family of Christians. His mother Emmelia was the daughter of a martyr and two of his brothers—Basil of Casearea and Peter of Sebaste—became bishops. His sister Macrina is a recognized saint of the Church. He studied rhetoric, married, and prepared for a secular career. Nevertheless, in time he embraced the priesthood and was consecrated a bishop about 371 by his brother St. Basil the Great and became Bishop of Nyssa, a small town on the river Halys, on the highway between Caesarea and Ancyra. After his ordination, he lived with his wife in a state of perpetual continency.

His episcopate was beset with problems, and a Synod of Nyssa in 376 deposed him, forcing him to remain in exile, until the death of the Emperor Valens. When Gratian ascended to the purple publishing an edict of tolerance, Gregory returned to Nyssa. He attended the Council of Constantinople in 381. He died in 385 or 386.

To give an idea of Gregory's strong belief in the Eucharist as the true Body and Blood of Christ, we quote from one of his many works, *The Great Catechism*.

> Rightly, then, do we believe that now also the bread which is consecrated by the Word of God is changed into the Body of God the Word. For that Body was once, by implication, bread, but has been consecrated by the inhabitation of the Word that tabernacled in the flesh.
>
> ...

Since, then, that God-containing flesh partook for its substance and support of this particular nourishment also, and since the God who was manifested infused Himself into perishable humanity for this purpose, viz. that by this communion with Deity mankind might at the same time be deified, for this end it is that, by dispensation of His grace, He disseminates Himself in every believer through that flesh, whose substance comes from bread and wine, blending Himself with the bodies of believers, to secure that, by this union with the immortal, man, too, may be a sharer in incorruption. He gives these gifts by virtue of the benediction through which He transelements the natural quality of these visible things to that immortal thing. (37).

Although he does not use the word transubstantiation, the thought is there. This is a beautiful expression of the true union that exists between Christ and those who receive His Body and Blood, which is the pledge of their eternal life. By partaking of the august mysteries of the altar, mortal man is given life that is eternal and immortal. He who is human is "deified," to use Gregory's word, by contact with the presence of Christ who comes to dwell in a special way in the souls of those who receive Him.

Another Bishop and Doctor of the Church who wrote about the Holy Eucharist is St. Ambrose (ca 340–397). History is not certain where he was born—Arles, Lyons, and Trier all claim him, but we do know that he descended from an ancient Roman family that counted both martyrs and high government officials among its members. His father, also named Ambrose or Ambrosius in Latin, a member of the senatorial aristocracy, was the Prefect of Gallia and the ruler of what is present day France, Britain, Spain, and Mauritania, Tingitana in Africa. This office was the highest that could be held by a Roman subject.

When Ambrosius, the elder, died about 354, the family moved to Rome. After completing an excellent liberal education there that included Greek, Ambrose took up the study of law and began his career as a lawyer. He entered the imperial service about 365. Because of his eloquence in court and his great success as a lawyer, he was appointed consular governor of Liguria and Æmilia in 371 with his headquarters at Mediolanum, present-day Milan.

As we have mentioned previously in this chapter, the Arian heresy that denied both the divinity of Christ and the doctrine of the Trinity was causing much turmoil in the Church. When the bishop of Milan died about 374, the question as to who would replace him—an Arian or a Catholic—caused a great deal of turmoil with a riot breaking out in the cathedral itself. As governor, Ambrose went to the cathedral and urged both sides to be peaceful, while not taking sides with either faction. In those days, bishops were elected by priests and people. Ambrose simply wanted them to conduct the proceedings without fighting.

As he was addressing the people in the cathedral, a voice cried, "Ambrose for bishop!" In short order, everyone in the cathedral—both Arians and Catholics—were chanting, "Ambrose for bishop!" They declared him their bishop by acclaim.

Ambrose, now about thirty-three years old, had a very successful career, a large estate, and a brilliant future ahead of him. He had no education or training to be a bishop and had not even been baptized. In those days many people put off baptism, because they wanted the complete forgiveness and remission of their sins that baptism confers at a later date when they were ready to adopt a life of virtue or face death. For example, Emperor Constantine was baptized on his deathbed.

Being a bishop in the days of Ambrose was a dangerous position to be in. Because the people had elected him as their bishop, and he wanted no part of it, he appealed to the emperor to overturn his election as Bishop of Milan, making the observation that he had not yet even been baptized. To escape from episcopal consecration, Ambrose went into hiding in the home of one of the Roman senators, who refused to hide him any longer, when he learned that the emperor applauded the idea of Ambrose becoming Bishop of Milan.

On December 7, 374, Ambrose was ordained a priest and consecrated a bishop, having been baptized only one week earlier. Serving faithfully as the Bishop of Milan until his death on April 4th, 397, Ambrose was a devoted shepherd of the flock of Christ. His secretary Paulinus relates that when anyone came to him to confession, he would weep openly so much so that the penitent would also weep. He had great trials, because the empress was Arian and tried to silence him. Shortly before his death Christ appeared to him. The Bishop of Vercelli gave him the Eucharist, and immediately after receiving it, he expired April 5, 397. His body rests in Milan in the basilica that he loved, together with the relics of two holy martyrs, Gervasius and Protasius, whose remains were discovered during his tenure.

Ambrose is famous for laying the foundation of hymnody in the Church, because when soldiers besieged his basilica, he stayed inside it with his people and had them sing the psalms. His writings are voluminous and have had great influence on the Church down through the centuries. In *De Mysteriis*, he wrote about the Holy Eucharist and explained also the mysteries of the faith concerning baptism and confirmation, for the instruction of those who were about to be received into the Church. Very clearly, he presents the doctrine of the Real Presence of Christ in the consecrated elements of bread and wine.

In Chapter VIII of *De Mysteriis*, Ambrose links the mysteries of the altar to the sacrifice of Melchisedech that foreshadowed it. He sets out to demonstrate that the rites of the altar are more ancient that those of the Jews and that the Eucharist is far better than the manna with which God fed His ancient people. He shows that Melchisedech, King of Righteousness and Peace, was a priest forever, and that he preceded Moses and the sacred rites of the Jews. As to comparing the Eucharist with manna, he points out that those who partook of manna all died, but that all who partake of the Holy Eucharist will live forever.

> But yet all those who ate that food died in the wilderness, but that food which you receive, that living Bread which came down from heaven, furnishes the substance of eternal life; and whosoever shall eat of this Bread shall never die, and it is the Body of Christ. (47)
>
> …
>
> Now consider whether the bread of angels be more excellent or the Flesh of Christ, which is indeed the body of life. That manna came from heaven, this is above the heavens; that was of heaven, this is of the Lord of the heavens; that was liable to corruption, if kept a second day, this is far from all corruption, for whosoever shall taste it wholly shall not be able to feel corruption. For them water flowed from the rock, for you Blood flowed from Christ; water satisfied them for a time, the Blood satiates you for eternity. The Jew drinks and thirsts again, you after drinking will be beyond the power of thirsting; that was in a shadow, this is in truth. (49)

In Chapter IX of this work, St. Ambrose seeks to convince his readers that the Eucharist is the true Body and Blood of Christ. He explains that the blessing over the elements, the epiclesis, changes them. (50)

> We observe, then, that grace has more power than nature, and, yet, so far we have only spoken of the grace of a prophet's blessing. But if the blessing of man had such power as to change nature, what are we to say of that divine consecration where the very words of the Lord and Savior operate? For that sacrament which you receive is made what it is by the word of Christ. But if the word of Elijah had such power as to bring down fire from heaven, shall not the word of Christ have power to change the nature of the elements? You read concerning the making of the whole world: "He spoke and they were made, He commanded and they were created." Shall not the word of Christ, which was able to make out of nothing that which was not, be able to change things which already are into what they were not? For it is not less to give a new nature to things than to change them. (59)

Speaking of the consecrated bread, St Ambrose observes: "It is the true Flesh of Christ which was crucified and buried; this is then truly the Sacrament of His Body" (63).

> The Lord Jesus Himself proclaims: "This is My Body." Before the blessing of the heavenly words, another nature is spoken of, after the consecration, the Body is signified. He Himself speaks of His Blood. Before the consecration, it has another name, after, it is called Blood. And you say, Amen, that is. It is true. Let the heart within confess what the mouth utters, let the soul feel what the voice speaks. (54)

St. Ambrose continues by speaking of the effects of the sacrament in the soul of the believer who receives it. It strengthens the substance of the soul and makes one to progress in grace. He insists that the mystery be not violated by evil deeds, nor should we share what is holy with unbelievers (55). He exhorts people to come to the sacrament of the altar.

> In that sacrament is Christ, because it is the Body of Christ, it is therefore not bodily food, but spiritual. Whence the Apostle says of its type: "Our fathers ate spiritual food and drank spiritual drink," for the Body of God is a spiritual body; the Body of Christ is the Body of the Divine Spirit, for the Spirit is Christ, as we read: "The Spirit before our face is Christ the Lord." And in the Epistle of Peter we read: "Christ died for us." Lastly, that food strengthens our heart, and that drink "makes glad the heart of man," as the prophet has recorded

Let us now consider the writings of St. Ambrose's famous convert St. Augustine, whose Latin name was Aurelius Augustinus, described by many as the greatest of the Fathers of the Western Church and called Doctor of Grace, because of his theological writings on the grace of God. He was born November 13, 354 in Roman North Africa in a town called Tagaste in Numidia, now present day Souk-Ahras in Algeria, not far from the ancient city of Carthage—now known as Tunis. His parents were Patricius, a pagan and burgess of Tagaste, and Monica—actually spelled Monnica—a Christian who tried to rear her son in the faith. Although he was enrolled as a catechumen of the Catholic Church, he was not baptized, as was the custom of many in those days. Once when he fell ill, he asked for baptism, but when the illness left him, so did any thought of being baptized.

Because Augustine excelled at learning, his father decided to educate him to become a rhetorician. When the boy had learned all he could in Tagaste, his father sent him to Madaura where he attended the public schools and learned the

Latin language. His native tongue was Punic. When he was only sixteen, he enrolled in the university at Carthage, where he was enthralled with the study of Latin literature, especially Cicero and Virgil. At Carthage, he also enjoyed the theater and social life. He and a woman, whose name he never reveals, began living together and were faithful to each other for about fifteen years. When Augustine was about eighteen years old, a son, whom he greatly loved, was born of this union—Adeodatus—meaning gift of God. Upon receiving his degree in rhetoric from the university, Augustine started teaching rhetoric. When he was about nineteen, he read Cicero's Hortensius and developed a burning love for truth that never left him. In this work, Cicero places wisdom and the pursuit of truth above the value of rhetoric. Augustine's search for truth led him to Manichaeism, a dualistic philosophy that posits a god of good and a god of evil. While he taught rhetoric in Tagaste, he also proclaimed Manichaeism to anyone who would listen. Because this philosophy could not help him deal with the grief he experienced upon the death of a friend, he became dissatisfied with it.

After a brief stay in Carthage, he moved to Rome and began a school of rhetoric there. When he was appointed Professor of Rhetoric to the Imperial Court, he moved to Milan and began attending the religious services of St. Ambrose, because he was greatly impressed by Ambrose's rhetoric and elegance of expression. From Ambrose, he learned to appreciate the Holy Scripture and how to interpret it allegorically. Listening to Ambrose he received the gift of faith.

Dissatisfied with his career, he left the court and took up residence in a country villa with his mother, his son, and some friends. At this time he was engaged in reading Plato, St. Paul, and the Neo-Platonists. One day, utterly distraught, he went into his garden and threw himself down under a fig tree, where, in a flood of uncontrollable tears, he poured out his soul to God. His soul was torn between embracing divine purity, the things of the world, and the pleasures of the flesh. He relates this event of his conversion in his *Confessions*.

> I flung myself down under a fig tree—how I know not—and gave free course to my tears. The streams of my eyes gushed out an acceptable sacrifice to You. And, not indeed in these words, but to this effect, I cried to You: "And You, O Lord, how long? How long, O Lord? Will You be angry forever? Oh, remember not against us our former iniquities." For I felt that I was still enthralled by them. I sent up these sorrowful cries: "How long, how long? Tomorrow and tomorrow? Why not now? Why not this very hour make an end to my uncleanness?"
>
> I was saying these things and weeping in the most bitter contrition of my heart, when suddenly I heard the voice of a boy or a girl—I know not which—coming from the neighboring house, chanting over and over again,

"Pick it up, read it; pick it up, read it." Immediately, I ceased weeping and began most earnestly to think whether it was usual for children in some kind of game to sing such a song, but I could not remember ever having heard the like. So, damming the torrent of my tears, I got to my feet, for I could not but think that this was a divine command to open the Bible and read the first passage I should light upon. For I had heard how Anthony, accidentally coming into church while the gospel was being read, received the admonition, as if what was read had been addressed to him: "Go and sell what you have and give it to the poor, and you shall have treasure in heaven; and come and follow me." By such an oracle he was forthwith converted to You. (29)

Immediately Augustine went to his mother who had been praying for years for his conversion and told her what had happened. This was in the summer of the year 386. At Easter of 387, Ambrose baptized him. Returning to Africa in 387, Augustine had no intention of becoming a priest. Knowing how Ambrose was elected to the episcopacy, he was careful to avoid being in cities that might be in need of a bishop, because he did not want to be similarly elected. However, one day in 391, he visited the town of Hippo, which he thought was safe, because they already had a bishop. As he listened to the Bishop of Hippo preach a homily, he was surprised to hear the bishop say that the Church needed priests and that he thought it would glorify God, if Augustine were ordained. Suddenly, people surrounded Augustine and unanimously chose him and took him up to the bishop who forthwith ordained him to the priesthood. Augustine was overwhelmed and broke into tears and wanted to escape, but was unable to. Later the Bishop of Hippo asked him to help serve the diocese as a coadjutor, which he did, and then upon the death of the bishop, Augustine succeeded him to the see of Hippo. From there he went on to become one of the greatest theologians the church has ever known, as attested by his voluminous writings. He died 28 August 430 at the age of 75.

In letter 98, dated in the year 408, to one Bishop Boniface, St. Augustine states that the Eucharist is a sacrifice, just as some of our earlier writers said, reflecting the universal belief of the Church in the sacrifice of the altar as the representation of the sacrifice of Christ on Calvary in an unbloody manner. He says:

Was not Christ once for all offered up in His own person as a sacrifice and yet, is He not likewise offered up in the sacrament as a sacrifice, not only in the special solemnities of Easter, but also daily among our congregations; so that the man who, being questioned, answers that He is offered as a sacrifice in that ordinance, declares what is strictly true? For if sacraments had not some points of real resemblance to the things of which they are the sacraments, they would not be sacraments at all. In most cases, moreover, they do in virtue of this likeness bear the names of the realities which they resemble. As, therefore, in a certain manner the sacrament of Christ's body is Christ's body, and the sacrament of Christ's blood is Christ's blood, in the same manner the sacrament of faith is faith. (9)

On Sunday October 23, at the altar of the martyr St. Cyprian, St. Augustine delivered a homily on John 6:54: "Then Jesus said to them: Amen, amen I say unto you: Except you eat the flesh of the Son of man, and drink his blood, you shall not have life in you." In explicating this text, Augustine wrote:

So then He both gave us of His Body and Blood a healthful refreshment, and briefly solved so great a question as to His Own Entireness. Let them then who eat, eat on, and them that drink, drink; let them hunger and thirst, eat Life, drink Life. That eating, is to be refreshed; but you are in such wise refreshed, as that that whereby you are refreshed, fails not. That drinking, what is it but to live? Eat Life, drink Life; you shall have life, and the Life is Entire. But then this shall be, that is, the Body and the Blood of Christ shall be each man's Life; if what is taken in the Sacrament visibly is in the truth itself eaten spiritually, drunk spiritually. For we have heard the Lord Himself saying, "It is the Spirit that quickens, but the flesh profits nothing. The words that I have spoken unto you are Spirit and Life. But there are some of you," says He, "that believe not." Such were they who said, "This is a hard saying, who can hear it?" It is hard, but only to the hard; that is, it is incredible, but only to the incredulous.

When we receive Christ in the Eucharist we receive Life—our Life—Christ becomes our Life. Augustine insists that we should adore Christ in the Eucharist prior to receiving Him. He makes it very clear that the Word of God sanctifies the bread on the altar so that it becomes the Body of Christ, and we who partake of it also become the Body of Christ. Here is how he expresses it:

I promised you who have been baptized a sermon in which I would explain the sacrament of the Lord's Table, which you now behold and which you became partakers of last night. You should understand what you have received, what you will receive, indeed what you should receive daily. The bread you see on the altar and that has been sanctified by the word of God is the Body of Christ. Through these things the Lord Christ wished to entrust to us his Body and his Blood which he shed for us unto the remission of sins. If you receive them well, you are that which you receive. The Apostle says: "One bread and we, the many, are one body."

Although we could write more about what St. Augustine has to say about the Holy Eucharist, we turn now to one of the greatest fathers of the Church in the East—St. John Chrysostom. The 'golden-mouthed" John of Antioch was born about 347 to a good family. His father Secundus, a commander in the imperial army, died when John was very young, leaving his mother Anthusa, who was only twenty, with the responsibility of rearing the child. When it became apparent that John had great intellectual abilities, it was decided that he would become a lawyer. When he was about eighteen years old, he was attracted to the lectures of Libanius, the tutor of St. Basil the Great, who in 354 had accepted the chair in rhetoric in Antioch. John became an eloquent lawyer with a brilliant future ahead of him. As he worked at the legal profession, he began to realize that the life of a lawyer was often at odds with the pure Christian doctrine he had learned from his mother.

Bishop Meletius of Antioch was impressed by the sterling qualities he saw in John, sought him out, befriended him, and prepared him for baptism, When John was about twenty-three years old, Meletius baptized him and then ordained him a lector.

After his baptism, John was a new creation, wanting to flee the world with his friend Basil and enter a monastery. However, because his mother protested so greatly, he decided to turn his home in which he lived with her into a monastery, where he practiced many austerities. Finally about the year 374, he left his mother's house and entered a monastic community in the mountains south of Antioch. Four years later he left the monastery to live in a cave, but, when after two years his health was greatly impaired, he had to return to Antioch.

After his return to Antioch, Bishop Meletius ordained him a deacon in 381. Flavian, the successor of Meletius, ordained John a priest in 386. The next twenty years he preached many sermons for which he is justly acclaimed, preaching twice a week on Saturdays and Sundays and during Lent and on Holy Days. His eloquence was greatly appreciated far and wide. When he preached in the cathedral, it was always densely crowded with people applauding him with much enthusiasm.

When, in September of 397, the Bishop of Constantinople died, the eunuch Eutropius, the prime minister of Emperor Arcadius, was to nominate the new bishop for the most illustrious see in the Church. Although there were many candidates for the bishopric, Eutropius had one in mind, because he had visited Antioch and had heard John preach and was very favorably impressed with him. Eutropius instructed one Asterius to kidnap John of Antioch and bring him the eight hundred miles to Constantinople. Asterius met with John in a chapel outside the walls of Antioch, where imperial officers took him prisoner. It was useless for John to protest. On February 26, 398, Theophilus, the Patriarch of Alexandria consecrated him Bishop of Constantinople.

When John moved into the house provided for him as the Bishop of Constantinople, he disposed of many of the rich furnishings there and gave the proceeds to the poor and the hospitals of the area. Eating his meals alone, he ate sparingly of plain food. Avoiding contact with the rich and the famous, he lived a simple life. Although the people liked him very much, he attracted the enmity of the court and the clergy, because he attacked their vices.

In due time, John began to feel the hatred of the Empress Eudoxia who contrived with the help of the Patriarch of Alexandria to have him banished. Because he alluded to her in one of his sermons with a reference to Queen Jezebel of the Bible, she was profoundly insulted, resenting being identified with the infamous evil queen. Consequently, John was arrested and taken into custody and removed from Constantinople. No sooner was he out of the city, when an earthquake occurred, causing Eudoxia to beg the Emperor to reverse John's banishment, because she thought she had displeased heaven by having him dismissed. John was returned to Constantinople, and the Partriarch of Alexandria left in disfavor.

Eudoxia and John apparently forgot their differences—for two months. When Eudoxia had a silver statue of herself erected in front of St. Sophia Church, there was so much noise at the dedication in September of 403 that it disturbed the religious services that were being held in the church. John stormed to the pulpit and blasted the empress by alluding to her as Herodias, the woman who demanded and got the head of John the Baptist on a platter. John's old enemies rallied to the cause of the empress. When an imperial officer went to the church to tell John to leave, he refused politely, saying that God had given him the church and only violence would make him leave. When about three thousand catechumens were to arrive for baptism at Easter, John went to the cathedral, as was his custom. When the emperor commanded guards to drag John from his cathedral, soldiers burst into the church with swords in their hands and spread throughout the building, driving the catechumens away from the baptismal font, injuring many so that the water in the baptismal font was stained with blood. The soldiers invaded the baptistry where women were in various states of undress. Entering the sanctuary, these pagans, it was said, handled the sacred elements of the altar. The soldiers even chased the priests, driving them from the church. Hastily assembled at the baths of Constantine where they were to be baptized, since they also were driven from the church, the catechumens were attacked by barbarian soldiers from Thrace that wounded the officiating priest on the head and struck the deacon so that he dropped the cruet of chrism. Then these Thracians took whatever they wished from the people and the church—jewelry, vestments, and altar vessels.

While John continued in residence in his episcopal palace, two attempts were made on his life. Finally on June 5, 404 when the emperor signed the edict banishing him, John surrendered together with two of his bishops who wanted to remain with him, as they put him on a ship and spirited him out of the city.

Eudoxia chose Cucusus a village on the borders of Cilicia and Lesser Armenia as the place of John Chrysostom's exile. He was taken there in the hottest season of the year, without any consideration being shown for his weakened condition, as they hurried as fast as they could. The journey was unbelievably severe. He was suffering with a fever. When his mule fell under his litter, they believed that John was dead and carried him over the mountains. He survived the trip and from the village in Armenia where he was exiled, he conducted an extensive correspondence, exerting great influence throughout the Church. Despite the severe winters, he continued to survive

Although Eudoxia preceded John in death, other enemies, hoping to hasten his death, determined that he would be transferred to a place that would be less congenial for him. They sent soldiers to take him from Cucusus to Comana, hoping that he would not survive the rigors of the journey. Sick with fever, John still managed to live during the three month trip, but was completely exhausted when they arrive at Comana. When they finally reached the area, they stopped at a chapel five or six miles from Comana to spend the night. The next morning they traveled about four miles, when the fever became so severe that they had to return to the chapel.

Then the following morning John went to the altar, wearing white baptismal robes, having given all his clothing away. He received the Body and Blood of Christ for the last time, saying: "Glory be to God for all things. Amen." These were his final words. He died September 14, 407 at the age of sixty. He was buried near Comana, but on January 27, 438, his body was transferred to Constantinople with great dignity and interred near the altar in the Church of the Holy Apostles, the place where the members of the imperial family were laid to rest. The emperor and his sister were present at the ceremony, praying that God would forgive their parents for the egregious injuries they had inflicted on the holy man of God.

John Chrysostom's belief in the Body and Blood of Jesus in the holy sacrament of the altar is clearly expressed in the Divine Liturgy written by him and celebrated in the churches of the East to this day.

I believe and confess, Lord, that You are truly the Christ, the Son of the living God, who came into the world to save sinners, of whom I am the first. I also believe that this is truly Your pure Body and that this is truly Your precious Blood. Therefore, I pray to You, have mercy upon me, and forgive my transgressions, voluntary and involuntary, in word and deed, known and unknown. And make me worthy without condemnation to partake of Your pure Mysteries for the forgiveness of sins and for life eternal. Amen.

In his homily on the eleventh chapter of I Corinthians, he also speaks about the Body and Blood of Jesus Christ. Commenting on the words of Apostle Paul, "The cup of blessing which we bless, is it not a communion of the Blood of Christ?" he writes:

This which is in the cup is that which flowed from His side, and of that do we partake. But he called it a cup of blessing, because holding it in our hands, we so exalt Him in our hymn, wondering, astonished at His unspeakable gift, blessing Him, among other things, for the pouring out of this self-same draught that we might not abide in error, and not only for pouring it out, but also for the imparting thereof to us all. "Wherefore if you desire blood," says He, "redden not the altar of idols with the slaughter of brute beasts, but My altar with My blood." Tell me, what can be more tremendous than this? What more tenderly kind? (24)

In a homily on Matthew chapter 26, he wrote expressing his belief in the real presence of Jesus in the sacrament of the altar.

How many now say, I would wish to see His form, the mark, His clothes, His shoes. Lo! You see Him! You touch Him! You eat Him! And you indeed desire to see His clothes, but He gives Himself to you, not to see only, but also to touch and eat and receive within you. Let then no one approach it with indifference, no one faint-hearted, but all with burning hearts, all fervent, all aroused. For if Jews standing, and having on their shoes and their staves in their hands, ate with haste, much more ought you to be watchful. For they indeed were to go forth to Palestine, wherefore also they had the garb of pilgrims, but you are about to remove unto Heaven.

John Chrysostom's work *On the Priesthood* has often been described as his most beautiful writing. As an example of this we cite a quotation from Book III.

For when you see the Lord sacrificed, and laid upon the altar, and the priest standing and praying over the victim, and all the worshippers empurpled with that precious blood, can you then think that you are still among men, and standing upon the earth? Are you not, on the contrary, straightway translated to Heaven, and casting out every carnal thought from the soul? Do you not with disembodied spirit and pure reason contemplate the things which are in Heaven? Oh! What a marvel! What love of God to man! He who sits on high with the Father is at that hour held in the hands of all, and gives Himself to those who are willing to embrace and grasp Him. And this all do through the eyes of faith. (4)

Writing in the same tradition as St. John Chrysostom, St. John Damascene, the last of the Greek Fathers, has given us a compendium of the belief of the Church in the East in his book *De Fide Orthodoxa, The Orthodox Faith*. He was born about the year 675 in Damascus to an Arab family. His father was a faithful Christian and the chief financial officer for the caliph Abdul Malek. When John was in his early twenties, his father looked for a teacher who could provide him with the best education possible. He discovered a Sicilian monk, Cosmas, who had been captured by Arabs in a raid in Italy. John's father, Mansur, liberated the monk and appointed him as tutor to John and his brother Cosmas. Under the tutelage of the Sicilian monk, John loved learning and progressed nicely.

When his father died, John became the chief councilor of Damascus. After he became embroiled in the iconoclast controversy, an enemy of his obtained a letter he had written, copied his signature from it, and affixed it to a letter, purportedly from John, offering to betray the city of Damascus into the hands of an enemy, and sent it to the caliph. The caliph would not believe John's protests of innocence and ordered his hand to be chopped off, since it had, the caliph believed, written the traitorous letter. When his hand was miraculously reattached, through the intercession of Mary, the Mother of Jesus, the caliph became convinced of John's innocence and wanted to reinstate him to his former position. Refusing the offer, John went with his brother to the monastery of St. Sabas, southeast of Jerusalem. In due time, John was ordained to the priesthood. He is one of the Doctors of the Church.

In *De Fide Orthodoxa*, he explains how the bread and the wine become the Body and Blood of Christ.

You ask how the bread becomes the Body of Christ and the wine and water the Blood of Christ, I shall tell you: the Holy Spirit comes upon them and accomplishes what surpasses every word and thought.

This is the body which is truly united to the Godhead, the same which is from the Blessed Virgin. This is not because that body which was taken up to heaven comes down from heaven, but because the very bread and wine are changed into the body and blood of God.

However, should you inquire as to the manner in which this is done, let it suffice for you to understand that it is by the Holy Spirit, just as it was of the Holy Virgin and by the Holy Spirit that the Lord, through and in Himself, took flesh. (4:13)

By the prayer known as the epiclesis, the bread and the wine become the Body and Blood, Soul and Divinity of Christ. To make himself perfectly clear John adds:

The bread and wine are not a figure of the body and blood of Christ—God forbid!—but the actual deified body of the Lord, because the Lord Himself said: "This is my body;" not "a figure of my body," but "my body," and not a figure of my blood," but "my blood."

John now continues his writing by urging everyone to approach the altar with a pure conscience and unwavering faith and with purity of body and soul.

Let us approach it with burning desire, and with our hands folded in the form of a cross, let us receive the body of the Crucified. With eyes, lips, and faces turned toward it, let us receive the divine burning coal, so that the fire of the coal may be added to the desire within us to consume our sins and enlighten our hearts, and so that by this communion of the divine fire we may be set afire and deified.

The faith of the Church from the very beginning is that the bread and the wine become the Body and Blood of Christ. In the ninth century some discussion occurred among theologians as to how the bread and the wine become the Body and Blood of Christ. At this time, the Church had not yet promulgated the doctrine of transubstantiation. Events occurred which led to the necessity of promulgating this dogma. Berengarius of Tours (ca 999–1088) became head of the school of St. Martin de Tours, and his teaching about the Eucharist attracted attention, because it was deemed false. King Henry I, titular Abbot of St. Martin of Tours, had Berengarius imprisoned. Then his doctrine concerning the Eucharist was examined and condemned at the Council of Vercelli (1050). The next year a national synod was held in Paris to judge Berengarius and his follower Eusebius Bruno, when both were condemned. At the Council of Tours (1055), Berengarius signed a statement that after the consecration, the bread and wine are truly the body and blood of Christ. Later at a council in Rome (1059), he recanted his statement and signed a statement of faith written by Cardinal Humbert in which he affirmed belief in the real and sensible presence of the body of Christ in the Eucharist. Shortly thereafter, Berengarius repudiated this statement and Eusebius Bruno deserted him. When the Count of Anjou and Geoffrey the Bearded forcefully opposed him, Berengarius appealed to Pope Alexander II who requested him to renounce his erroneous beliefs about the Eucharist. With contempt, Berengarius refused to accede to the pope's request. He was condemned again by the Councils of Poitiers (1075) and St. Maixeut (1076). In 1078, Pope Gregory VII ordered him to come to Rome. In a council held in St. John Lateran, he signed a statement affirming the changing of the bread into the body of Christ, born of the Virgin Mary. At a second council held at the Lateran in 1079, Berengarius signed a statement of faith, which resembled the one he signed the previous year, but was more explicit. Pope Gregory VII recommended Berengarius to the bishops of Tours and Angers, stating that no penalty was to be imposed on him and that no one was to call him heretical. Before long, however, he attacked the statement he had signed at the Lateran. However, he made a final retraction as a result of a Council held at Bordeaux in 1080. He went into solitude on the island of St. Cosme and died in union with the Church.

Because Berengarius brought forth and taught heretical doctrines, it became necessary for the Church to explain exactly what takes place at the consecration of the bread and wine. The result was the promulgation of the doctrine of transubstantiation. By transubstantiation, the substance of bread is converted into the Body of Christ and the substance of wine into the Blood of Christ. In other words, bread and wine are essentially converted into the Body and Blood of Christ. In transubstantiation only the substance is converted and the accidents—the appearances of bread and wine—are not converted, but remain the same. For example, if there were a way to convert a piece of iron into a block of wood and retain the appearances of iron—that would be transubstantiation. The substance is converted, but the accidents which give it the appearance of iron remain the same. The doctrine is very explicitly defined by the Council of Trent that as a consequence of transubstantiation the entire substance of the bread and wine are converted into the Body and Blood of Christ (Sess. XIII, can. ii).

Hildebert of Lavardin, Bishop of Le Mans and Archbishop of Tours (ca 1056–ca 1134) is the first person to use the word transubstantiation. The Council of Rome that condemned Berengarius is the first document to express clearly that a substantial change takes place at the consecration. St. Thomas Aquinas defines transubstantiation in the Summa (III, Q. lxxv, a.4). It is most likely that the feast of Corpus Christi was instituted as a result of the controversies that took place over the Eucharist. These controversies are also probably responsible for the Host being elevated after the consecration in the Mass.

When the Protestants left the Church at the time of the Reformation, they lost the Holy Eucharist because they were unable to maintain apostolic succession. Without apostolic succession—the process by which bishops have consecrated other bishops in a direct line that goes back to the apostles—they were unable to have a validly ordained priesthood. Without the priesthood, there could be no validly consecrated Eucharist. For this reason most of the Protestants simply regard the grape juice and bread they pass out in little cups and baskets for their communion as simply a memorial of the Lord. The Anglicans have tried to reestablish the apostolic succession that was broken at the time of Henry VIII and Elizabeth I and claim to have done so. They have been able to get bishops from schismatic groups who have apostolic succession to participate in their ordinations. However, Rome has made the definitive pronouncement that their orders are not valid. Even though the Eastern Orthodox Church has cordial relations with the Anglican Communion, they would require an Anglican priest who converted to Orthodoxy to be ordained again by them. The Eastern Orthodox, having valid apostolic succession, believe that the bread and the wine, when consecrated are the Body and Blood of Jesus, just as St. John Damascene has written. However, they do not use the word "transubstantiation," because they have not been plagued by any controversies about the Eucharist that would have necessitated the definition, as to how the consecration changes the elements of bread and wine into the Body and Blood of Christ. They simply leave the mystery undefined and understand it as did St. John Damascene. Throughout the history of the Church, the promulgation of dogmas has resulted when doctrines have been questioned and there has been confusion about them. Since the Church has very definitively promulgated the doctrine of transubstantiation at the Council of Trent, there should be no more controversy about it among Catholics.

Sadly to say, there are those in the Church today that have lost faith in transubstantiation or else they do not know what it signifies. During the years since Vatican II, catechism has been greatly neglected in the instruction of the young. A whole generation has grown up not realizing the truth about the Holy Eucharist. It is to help these people that this chapter has been written.

After we have read the wonderful things the Greek and Latin Fathers of Church have written about the Eucharist and how it is truly the Body and Blood of the Risen Lord, it is hard to understand the unfavorable manner in which some today regard the Eucharist. It is very painful to hear some of them refer to adoration of the Sacred Host at Benediction as "Cookie Worship." What could be more contemptuous than that? May they come to learn what great treasure this sacrament is and begin to make restitution to the Lord of Glory for the way they have treated Him. The Saints of the Church have always regarded Holy Communion as the way to the highest mystical union with Christ. We can learn much from them on how to approach the altar of God to receive Him. To anyone who sincerely desires to learn about how to receive the Body and Blood of Christ we recommend *The Imitation of Christ*, as a starting place. This book was written by Thomas à Kempis who was born at Kempen in the Diocese of Cologne circa 1379 or 1380 and died 25 July, 1471. This little classic has formed souls down through the centuries and is an excellent place to get started with Eucharistic devotion. Once one has been able to discern the Body and Blood of Christ in the Eucharist, no book can be an instructor, for the Holy Spirit is the One who leads and guides those who place themselves in His keeping.

The *Imitation of Christ* is a delightful little book that tucks neatly into one's pocket. It is available in all bookstores and for free distribution on the internet in the Gutenberg Project. It consists of four parts or books, the fourth dealing with the Sacrament of the Altar. It begins with a devout exhortation to Holy Communion and is a dialogue between the soul and Christ. We present here a sample of this work to entice our readers to read it and pray it.

> Angels and Archangels stand in awe of You, the Saints and just men fear You, and You say, Come unto Me! Except You, Lord, had said it, who should believe it true? And except You had commanded, who should attempt to draw near?
>
> Oh admirable and hidden grace of the Sacrament, which only Christ's faithful ones know, but the faithless and those who serve sin cannot experience! In this Sacrament is conferred spiritual grace, and lost virtue is regained in the soul, and the beauty which was disfigured by sin returns again. So great sometimes is this grace that out of the fullness of devotion given, not only the mind but also the weak body feels that more strength is supplied unto it.
>
> Oh wonderful condescension of Your pity surrounding us, that You, O Lord God, Creator and Quickener of all spirits, deign to come unto a soul so poor and weak, and to appease its hunger with Your whole Deity and Humanity. Oh happy mind and blessed soul, to which is granted devoutly to receive You its Lord God, and in so receiving You to be filled with all spiritual joy!
>
> Oh how great a Lord does it entertain, how beloved a Guest does it bring in, how delightful a Companion does it receive, how faithful a Friend does it welcome, how beautiful and exalted a Spouse, above every other Beloved, does it embrace, One to be loved above all things that can be desired!

Oh my most sweet Beloved, let heaven and earth and all the glory of them, be silent in Your presence; seeing whatsoever praise and beauty they have it is of Your gracious bounty; and they shall never reach unto the loveliness of Your Name, Whose Wisdom is infinite

If you had angelic purity and the holiness of holy John the Baptist, you would not be worthy to receive or to minister this Sacrament. For this is not deserved by merit of man that a man should consecrate and minister the Sacrament of Christ, and take for food the bread of Angels. Vast is the mystery, and great is the dignity of the priests, to whom is given what is not granted to Angels. For priests only, rightly ordained in the Church, have the power of consecrating and celebrating the Body of Christ. The priest indeed is the minister of God, using the Word of God by God's command and institution; nevertheless God is there the principal Author and invisible Worker, that to whom all that He wills is subject, and all He commands is obedient.

Hopefully this little book will teach you devoutly and reverently to receive the Body and Blood of Christ, so that having learned from it you will be able to let the Holy Spirit lead you in higher paths to union with Christ.

"Heavenly Father, we thank You for sending us Jesus to lift us up to you. Most Blessed Savior, we thank you for shedding all Your blood to save us. Holy Spirit, we thank you for leading us to Jesus. Teach us how faithfully and devoutly to receive His most precious Body and Blood. Amen"

16

The Prince of Peace

If we would find peace, we must go to the Prince of Peace. Only He can give us what the world cannot—true and lasting peace. Long before His birth, the prophet Isaiah announced His coming: "For a child is born to us, and a son is given to us, and the government is upon his shoulder, and his name shall be called, Wonderful, Counselor, God the Mighty, the Father of the world to come, the Prince of Peace" (9:6). Much later when the angel Gabriel appeared to Mary, announcing to her that she would have a son called Jesus, he told her, "He shall be great, and shall be called the Son of the Most High; and the Lord shall give unto Him the throne of David His father, and He shall reign in the house of Jacob forever" (Lk 1:32). When the angels announced His birth the first Christmas, they sang, "Glory to God in the highest; and on earth peace to men of good will" (Lk 2:14).

Our God is a God of peace. St Paul frequently refers to him as the God of peace. He writes "Now the God of peace be with you all" (Ro 15:33). In II Corinthians, he tells the people: "Brethren, rejoice, be perfect, take exhortation, be of one mind, have peace; and the God of peace and of love shall be with you" (13:11).

When Adam and Eve disobeyed God, sin began to abound on the earth. Cain killed his brother Abel, and, with the passing of time, there was so much iniquity in the world that the Lord decided to destroy the human race, with the exception of Noah and his family. Then for some mysterious reason, God appeared to Abram, changed his name to Abraham, and promised that everyone would be blessed by his countless descendants. With the descendants of Abraham, God fashioned a people that belonged especially to Him. Through the prophets, He began to speak to them, promising them a Messiah, who would come and save them from their sins and bring peace—peace between God and man, and peace among men. Ever since Adam and Eve sinned, men have done the evil they did not want to do and have left undone the things they ought to have done.

God told Adam and Eve that on the day they ate the forbidden fruit that they would die. But God is good. He turned the sin of Adam and Eve into what the Church calls *felix culpa*—or happy fault. Because of their sin, He determined to send a Redeemer who would atone for the wrong of our first parents. He sent His son as the Prince of Peace to restore the closeness that existed between man and God, before sin came into the world, and to bring peace between heaven and earth. The Church refers to the sin of Adam and Eve as a happy fault, because with the redemption God planned for them, they would be raised to a higher state than they would have been, if they had never sinned in the first place. All things work together for good for those who love God and are called according to His purposes—even sins (Ro 8:28).

God would send His Son, the Second Person of the Blessed Trinity, to be incarnated as a man. God would become a man and as a man, He would atone for sin. Not only would He atone for sin by His death on the cross, He would arrange for His Divine Life to enter into man. He would unite humanity to the Godhead in a hypostatic union that would endure forever. Jesus is God in human flesh—One Person with two natures—one human, one divine. As the Fathers of the Church have said, God became a man, that man might be divinized and share in the life of God.

As we grow in closer union with Jesus, we enter more fully into His Life. He becomes our Life. As we receive the Prince of Peace in Holy Communion, we receive our Life and we become filled with peace—peace that passes all understanding. We let Him guide us and direct us, doing the things that please Him. He tells each believer: "If you love me, keep my commandments." As we keep His commandments, we grow in holiness and closer to Him, to the Heavenly Father, and to the Holy Spirit—the Three Persons of God. Just as John the Baptist said, He must increase, we must decrease.

As He increases within us and our selfish egocentric ways give way to His love, we breathe in His peace, and our hearts are filled with love for Him and for our friends and neighbors. Then it becomes easier for us to keep His commandments—because we love. We become the beloved children of God who reflect the glory of Jesus in our lives. We are filled with radiant LIFE—life that will never end.

Jesus tells us that this is eternal life—that we may know the Heavenly Father, the only true God, and Jesus Christ whom He has sent (Jn 17:3). If we know Him, we already possess eternal life. We are already in eternal life. Jesus tells us that the one who hears His Word, and believes the One who sent Him to us—the Heavenly Father—has life everlasting, and comes not into judgment, but is passed from death to life (Jn 5:24).

Jesus also tells us that in His Father's house there are many mansions. The kind of mansion we will receive in the life of the world to come will depend upon how faithfully we have corresponded to and cooperated with the grace that He has given us in this life and how much love is in our souls when we pass from this life to the next.

Jesus also tells us to lay up treasures in heaven. "Lay not up to yourselves treasures on earth, where the rust, and moth consume, and where thieves break through and steal, but lay up to yourselves treasures in heaven, where neither the rust nor moth does consume, and where thieves do not break through, nor steal, for where your treasure is, there is your heart also. (Mt 6:19–21). How do we lay up treasure in heaven? We let the Prince of Peace fill our hearts with His peace and love and then share it with all those we meet each day. Love is the coin of the realm of heaven. The one who is richest in heaven is the one who loves the most.

How do we learn love? By doing the spiritual and corporal works of mercy. We bear wrongs patiently, forgive offences willingly, comfort the afflicted, pray for the living and the dead, instruct the ignorant, counsel those in doubt, and admonish sinners. These are the spiritual works of mercy. The corporal works of mercy are these. We feed the hungry, give drink to those that thirst, clothe the naked, shelter those who have no shelter, visit the sick, ransom the captive, bury the dead.

We do not always have an opportunity to practice all of these works of mercy. We do what we can. Most of us do not have an opportunity to ransom captives. However, two religious congregations have been founded to do just that. St. John of Matha and St. Felix of Valois founded the Trinitarians in 1198 for that purpose. In 1218, St. Peter Nolasco and St. Raymond of Pennafort started the Order of Our Lady of Ransom to ransom Christians who were held captive by the Muslims. In the Order of Our Lady of Ransom, the members took a fourth vow—they would surrender themselves in place of people they could not otherwise set free. Obviously they are following the teaching of Jesus that no one has greater love than he who lays down his life for someone else.

As St. Therese of Lisieux said, holiness does not take much time—it takes much love. How can we get this kind of love which transfigures us and makes us radiantly alive and beautiful? We ask God to give it to us. Love is His gift to us. It is an infused virtue. Let us beseech Him daily to increase His love in our hearts so that we can love Him and all our brothers and sisters in Christ with His own love.

As we pray for Him to increase His love in our souls, we should also pray for an increase of the infused virtues of faith and hope, for the three—faith, hope and love—grow together in the human soul. An increase of faith brings an increase of hope and an increase of love. We cannot have too much faith, too much hope, or too much love. They are the virtues that unite us to God and fill us with His divine Life.

As we grow in love, we will find that it become easier to keep His commandments. As St. Augustine said centuries ago, "Love God and do what you will." If we truly love God, we will not do anything that displeases Him." Love is the only way to holiness. Holiness is wholeness, completeness. We shall not experience this completeness in this life, but only in the next when our glorified bodies will be reunited with our souls.

St. Paul tells us: "That eye hath not seen, nor ear heard, neither hath it entered into the heart of man, what things God has prepared for them that love him. But to us God has revealed them by this Spirit. For the Spirit searches all things, yea, the deep things of God (I Co 2:9). Our faith teaches us that, in the beatific vision in the life of the world to come, we shall possess God. The beatific vision will produce beatific love in us. Then we shall be like Him, for we shall see Him as He is (I Jn 3:2). St. Paul explains; "We see now through a glass in a dark manner, but then face to face (I Co 13:12). Now we know in part, then we shall know Him even as we are known.

Speaking of the Light of Glory, Garrigou LaGrange writes;

> This vision, intuitive and immediate, reaches the object of that uncreated vision whereby God knows Himself. It reaches Him less perfectly than He does Himself, but it reaches Him. (*Life* 225–226)

This happens because a supernatural light elevates the soul.

> This light, received in a permanent fashion in the intellects of the blessed, is called the light of glory, The Council of Vienne condemns those who "maintain that the human soul does not have to be elevated by the light of glory in order to see God and have holy joy in Him." (226)

Garrigou-Lagrange goes on to explain: "This light supernaturalizes the vitality of our intelligence, as the infused virtue of charity supernaturalizes the vitality of our will" (226). The light of glory and infused charity of heaven come from the consummation of sanctifying grace.

What will we see in the beatific vision? According to this theologian we will see God's essence, His attributes, and the Three Persons of the Trinity (127). He also says that the first glimpse of the beatific vision will last forever. "Heaven's joy is an everlasting morning" (237). The degree of our beatitude in Eternity will depend on the degree of our merits and our love at the moment of our death.

Garigou-Lagrange also tells us that part of our beatitude in heaven will come from loving other people. The closer people are to God, the more we will love them, but we will have special affection for those we have loved in this life (245). Our essential beatitude will be in the beatific vision of God, but our accidental beatitude will consist in enjoying the company of our friends (247).

What will our glorious resurrected bodies be like? Garrigou-Lagrange explains the teaching of the Church on this subject. The body will be perfectly subjected to the soul and will never experience pain or death again. The body will be very agile and be able to go swiftly wherever the soul wishes. Like Christ who penetrated the room where the apostles were, when the doors were closed, we will be able to penetrate other objects. Our bodies will be resplendent like Our Lord's, when He was transfigured on Mt. Tabor. The glory of the soul will flood the body making it beautiful and radiant. The greater the soul's light of glory, the more resplendent the body will be (254).

How do we know that we are on the way to heaven? Are we living in grace? The first sign is that we have accepted Jesus as our Lord and Savior and try to keep His commandments. If we have been born again, repented of our sins, confessed them, and receive Christ in Holy Communion, we are on the right road. We are learning to hate sin and avoid it. Once we enter into a personal relationship with Jesus, we love the things He loves and hate evil. We begin to realize the things that are wrong in our lives. We either love God and hate sin, or love sin and hate God. We have to decide whether we will choose life or choose death. Some people receive the grace to change their lives almost instantly, while others struggle with sin for a long time. It is a sign that we are on the way to heaven, if we love what is good and hate evil.

When we receive God's salvation into our souls we begin to feel awe in His presence, because we begin to realize how great and good He is. When we come into His presence, we experience something that we could never have felt, when we were living in sin. We begin to understand more and more of the goodness and love of God.

If we do not experience anything of the presence of God—if religion and church are boring for us, we need to examine our souls to see what we are doing that is wrong. We should ask Jesus to come into our hearts and save us. If we do experience joy in the presence of the Lord, then we are walking on the way that leads to heaven.

Another sign that we are on the way to heaven is if we love the Word of God. The better friends we become with Jesus, the more we want to know what He has to say to us in His Word. If we thirst for the Word of God, that is a sign that we are headed for heaven. We have already begun to rejoice in Him, and our rejoicing will last forever.

A sure sign that we are headed for heaven is if we love our brothers and sisters in Christ. If we love the people of God, we are living in grace and on the royal road that leads to God and heaven. Only God knows if we have true love in our hearts. We know that we have passed from death to life, if we love our brethren (Jn 3:14). If we have this sign, we can be sure that we are going to heaven. Love in our hearts is a great sign that we are heaven bound. Our Prince of Peace will come at the hour death to take us home to the mansion he has prepared for us. He will say, "Welcome, good and faithful servant, into the joy of the Lord." We will have an eternity of peace, love, and joy!

"Heavenly Father, we thank You that You sent us the Prince of Peace to draw us to You and fill our hearts with His love and peace. We want to be holy and pleasing in Your sight. We are thankful that Jesus has made us your adopted sons and daughters. Lord Jesus, we want to be like You and see You as You are. Holy Spirit, draw us to Jesus and with Your grace make us like Him. Holy Trinity of Love, we long to behold the vision of You forever. In Jesus name we pray, Amen."

17

Prayer Brings Peace

When life swirls around us at its most furious pace and we have more to do than we can possibly get done, and our strength seems to be failing, what *do* we do? How do we cope? Here is what Holy Scripture tells us: "in silence and in hope shall your strength be" (Is 30:15). We need to be still and enter into our souls where the Lord of Peace is always present. He tells us in the words of the psalmist, "Be still and see that I am God!" (Ps 45:11). There is always calm in the midst of the storms of life, if we enter into the presence of the Lord and hope in Him, for the winds and the waves obey His commands. In a few moments of prayer, we can regain our composure and assess the situation in which we find ourselves. Then what do we do? We do the next thing—whatever comes next. In this way, we can sort out the confusion and remove it from our minds and get on with our life—by doing whatever comes next, not worrying about everything at once, but by taking things one step at a time.

It is impossible to deal with life, if we do not pray. Prayer will bring peace to the most troublesome situations if we simply put everything in the hands of the Lord—if we hope in Him and seek His presence. We must trust in His loving Providence to care for us, as He cares for the birds of the air and the lilies of the valley. He has brought us thus far, and He will see us safely home with Him in glory, if we simply trust and obey. He knows our needs, even before we ask Him for them in prayer, but He still wants us to ask.

Jesus tells us that if we ask, we will receive. In His Sermon on the Mount, He tells us to seek, and we shall find, ask, and it shall be given to us, to knock, and the way will be made open for us. He reminds us that we, as parents, give good gifts to our children, and that God who is infinitely good gives good gifts to His children. When we pray we have to ask in faith, believing that we will receive what we need. We do not get everything we want, but we do get all our needs provided for. God takes care of His children. The Word of God tells us through the psalmist: "I have been young, and now am old; and I have not seen the just forsaken, nor his seed seeking bread" (Ps 36:25). St. Paul tells us that God "is able to do all things more abundantly than we desire or understand, according to the power that works in us" (Ep 3:20). The Apostle James tells that we must ask in faith without any wavering, for if we waver we are like a wave of the sea that is moved hither and yon by the wind, and we shall not receive anything from the Lord (Jm 1:6–7).

Because the Lord Himself tells us that when two of us Christians are in agreement, the Heavenly Father will do what we ask, it is a good practice to have a prayer partner who will agree with us in presenting our petitions to God. To have our prayers answered we must learn to pray effectively. This does not mean that we have to compose elegant sounding prayers that are long and repetitious. Rather we must pray from the heart in all simplicity. We must be instant in prayer; we must pray continually. If we will live in close union with Christ, the work we do must become a prayer.

There are a number of things that can impede our prayer from rising to the throne of God—among them are sin, ingratitude, and the failure to forgive those who have offended us. Sin clouds the surface of our souls with a dark impenetrable film that our prayers cannot pierce, if the sins are mortal. Venial sins are like dust that can be blown away, if we make fervent acts of love towards God and other people. We need to be in a right relationship with God, if we want Him to answer our prayers. The Apostle James tells us that sometimes we do not receive from God when we ask, because our petitions are wrong, in that we ask for things that will just satisfy the desires of the flesh (Jm 4:3). If our prayer is not in the will of God, it will not be granted to us.

How do we know that we pray in the will of God? If we pray the way Our Lord taught us to pray in the Our Father, we can be sure we are praying correctly. This prayer, apparently simple, but really very complex in its content, should be our guide. Our Father, who art in heaven, hallowed be Your name. Your kingdom come. Your will be done on earth as it is in heaven. Give us this day our daily bread. And forgive us our debts, as we forgive our debtors. And lead us not into temptation. But deliver us from evil. Amen.

Jesus taught us to address God as "Father," but this is possible only because Jesus identifies so completely with the members of His mystical body that we are one with Him. God is our Father only if we have Jesus for our Lord and Savior. He is our elder brother whose shed blood makes us children of God and infuses our souls with divine life. It is because Jesus has made us new creatures in Him by baptism that we can call God "Our Father."

"Who art in heaven" reminds us that while God is everywhere present, the blessed in the realms of glory, to which company we are called, are with Him in a special way. Heaven is His throne and earth His footstool. We also know that Jesus told us that the kingdom of heaven is within us. Heaven is in our souls, because God is there. We lift up our hearts to Him who is present within. We draw near to Him with confidence, knowing that He will provide for all our necessities. As we draw nearer to Him, He draws closer to us. We experience His presence, and we adore Him, saying hallowed be Your name, joining in with the Trisagion of the angels. Jesus has opened the door of God's presence to us, making us a royal priesthood, a nation of prophets, priests, and kings. God is always on the throne of our hearts waiting to hear from us.

"Hallowed be Your name" means may God's name be glorified. We praise Him and give Him glory, as soon as we place ourselves in His presence and before we begin any petitions. Here we must comment on the fact that we pray, "Our Father," not "My Father." We are an ecclesial community and we pray as one to our Father God, for we are God's people that He has called out of the rest, for the praise and glory of His name.

Jesus is our great High Priest who lives always to make intercession for us to the throne of grace. He always hears us, for He and the Holy Spirit, together with the Heavenly Father dwell within us, if we are in a state of grace. He wants us to have utter confidence in Him. He knows us better than we know ourselves. He tells us that the very strands of hair on heads are numbered. Nothing is hidden from His sight, but He loves us in spite of our failures and imperfections. He even takes our sins and brings good from them.

When we pray "hallowed be Thy name" we should remember the beautiful name of the Savior—Jesus—and always strive to honor it. It is the name of our salvation. St. Luke tells us this: "For there is no other name under heaven given to men, whereby we must be saved." (Ac 4:12) His name is so wonderful that He promises us: "If you shall ask me anything in My name—that I will do" (Jn 14:14). But we must ask in accordance with His will. We cannot expect to get things that are not good for us, or just satisfy our selfish pleasure. We need to pray for things that will glorify God and further His kingdom.

And so we pray, "Your kingdom come." We pray that our hearts may be transformed by His love and that through us He will extend His kingdom throughout the whole earth. We know from Scripture that He wills all men to be saved and for that to happen the kingdom must come to all. We cannot do this on our own; only His grace can help us build the kingdom here on earth, as it is in heaven. "Your will be done on earth, as it is in heaven." With this petition we ask Him to touch our hearts and make them like His own, so that we may be transformed and radiate His glory, so that those who have not yet entered the kingdom will see His beauty in us and embrace Him. If we ask Him, He will give us the grace to enable us to keep His commandments and do His will on earth, as the angels do it in heaven. He will give us power through the Holy Spirit to rise to heights we have never even dreamed were possible.

"Give us this day our daily bread" our prayer continues. Notice we are praying for *our* bread—for the bread of our entire ecclesial community. And what is that bread? We are asking for God to feed us with the Holy Eucharist—His holy presence in our midst. We are asking Him to feed us each day with His Body and Blood. May there always be priests to confect the Eucharist and feed the flock, so that the flickering candle in the sanctuary will always burn brightly, letting us know that He is with us on the altar. The Eucharist is the very Life of the Church and of her members.

We are also praying with this petition that the Lord will fill us with the divine life of the Holy Spirit with all His gifts and fruits, making it possible for us to glorify Him. We are asking that He will feed us with His Word that we may grow daily closer to Him. We know that He will answer this petition and grant us what we ask, for He has promised that the gates of hell shall never prevail against His Church, and that He will be with us always until the consummation of the world.

The next petition of the Our Father is especially important, although some people seem to rush over it without giving it much thought. "Forgive us our debts, as we forgive our debtors" indicates to us that if we want God to forgive our sins, we must forgive those who have offended us. Some people will never enter into the kingdom, because they want to hold on to past grievances, insults, and offenses. They simply refuse to forgive. Happiness is found only by those who forgive. Our mercy must be like that of God. The psalmist tells us that His mercy endures for ever. Jesus says we are to forgive seventy times seven—an infinite number. Forgiveness brings peace, because when we forgive others, we ensure that God will forgive us, and our hearts are at peace. Unfortunately nowadays, many people seem to have abandoned the Sacrament of Penance or Reconciliation. What could bring more peace than to hear the Lord speaking though His priest, saying "I absolve you in the name of the Father, the Son, and the Holy Spirit?"

The Lord's Prayer continues as we ask: "Lead us not into temptation." We know that we will encounter many trials and difficulties in this life, and we beseech God to help us in overcoming them all. We need His grace if we are going to live triumphant and victorious Christian lives. Left to our own devices, we would fail miserably, but we do not have to worry, for Christ is always with us, directing our steps, so that we may never fall into sin.

"Deliver us from evil" is the petition with which we ask God to protect us from all evil—physical as well as spiritual. May He protect us as we drive on the highway. May He watch over us when danger threatens and help us. May His prevenient grace shield us from all harm. May we thank Him for all the times in the past when He has kept us safe in body and soul, when we were not even aware that danger lurked in our midst. May He defend us from all the attacks of the enemy and keep us ever close to Him.

We conclude this prayer, saying, "For Yours is the power and the glory forever. Amen." The Church added this doxology to the Lord's Prayer at a very early time in her history. We praise God for His majesty and glory, for we are a people of praise.

To help us with a personal prayer liturgy, we offer the following: Before we begin formal prayer—we pray always informally in the secret recesses of our hearts—we retire to a suitable place where we can be alone with the Lord. It does not matter where our prayer place might be. Wherever we are most comfortable and find it easiest to pray is the proper place. This can be on the back porch, out in the forest—if we live in the country—or perhaps in the bathtub, or even lying in bed. The ideal place to go to pray is in the church before the Blessed Sacrament.

It is a wonderful practice to visit Jesus in the Reserved Eucharist every day for about thirty minutes. We can slip quietly into the church, knowing that He is there waiting for us. It seems easy to talk to Him as we kneel before the tabernacle, with the sanctuary light glowing red in the shadows of the church. However, wherever we pray, we first need to put ourselves in the presence of God. It is just easier to do that kneeling before the altar.

We begin our prayer with acts of thanksgiving and praise, which should rise spontaneously in our hearts. There is so much to thank Him for. "Lord, thank you for the beautiful day today. Praise you for the wonderful happy day you have given us." We can thank Him for simple things. "Thank you Lord for helping us to find a parking place this morning. And the fresh peaches that are now ripe are very nice—praise you and thank you for them." Everything in our lives is something we can thank and praise Him for.

Next we make acts of faith, hope, and love. We can use the prayers in the prayer book for this—it is easy to memorize them—or we can improvise and say, "I believe in You, Lord and all Your Word teaches about You. I hope in You for grace to take me securely through this life and get me safely to heaven some day. I love You with all my being and I love my brothers and sisters in You.

Having prayed thus, we should be beginning to be aware of God's presence. Now it is time for us just to be still and listen to what He has to say in our hearts. We might say, "Speak Lord, for Your servant hears," using the words of Samuel, when the Lord was trying to communicate with Him (I Sa 3:10). We do not expect Him to speak to us in words—experiences of that kind are very rare. We look for His inspirations in the quiet recesses of our minds and hearts. He will put them there. He will fill us with good thoughts and give us ideas about how to handle the things than concern us. When we have finished with this part of our prayer—and it can last a long time as we commune in silence with Him—we pray the Our Father, the Hail Mary, and the Gloria. We thank Him for sharing our prayer time with us and listening to us, anticipating that He will grant any requests we may have made. We spend the rest of our prayer time praising Him. The psalms are the best way to praise Him. Perhaps we might memorize one or two for this purpose. It is very acceptable to praise Him with a psalm because they are the Word of God.

We might try another praise prayer of the Church—the *Te Deum Laudamus*. This glorious hymn of praise, written well over fifteen hundred years ago, is one that glorifies God very beautifully. In the old Roman Breviary it is found at the end of Matins for Sunday and is called "Hymnus SS. Ambrosii et Augustini." According to tradition, the *Te Deum* was composed spontaneously and sung, alternating verses, by St. Ambrose and St, Augustine, on the night Ambrose baptized Augustine in 387 A. D. Others attribute it to St. Cyprian of Carthage and cite the year 252 as being when he composed it, during an outbreak of the plague. We cannot be sure who wrote it, but it is from antiquity. For those who are not familiar with it we quote it here in its entirety and end this chapter with it.

> We praise Thee, O God, we acknowledge Thee to be the Lord. All the earth doth worship Thee, the Father Everlasting! To Thee all angels cry aloud, the heavens and all they that dwell therein.
>
> To thee the Cherubim and Seraphim continually do cry "Holy, Holy, Holy, Lord God of Sabaoth, Heaven and earth are full of the majesty of thy glory!"
>
> The glorious choir of the Apostles praises thee. The wondrous company of prophets praises thee. The noble army of martyrs praises thee. The Holy Church throughout the world doth acknowledge thee, the Father of an infinite majesty and Thine own adorable, true, and only Son, also the Holy Spirit, the Comforter

Thou art the King of Glory, O Christ! Thou art the everlasting son of the Father. When Thou tookest it upon Thyself to deliver man, Thou didst humble thyself to be born of a virgin, overcoming the sting of death, Thou didst open the kingdom of heaven to all believers. Thou sittest at the right hand of God the Father in glory.

We believe that thou willst come to be our judge We therefore implore thee to help thy servants whom thou hast redeemed with Thy precious blood. Make them to be numbered among thy saints in glory everlasting.

Save thy people, O Lord, and bless Thine inheritance. Govern them and lift them up forever. Day by day we thank Thee, and we praise Thy name forever and ever.

O Lord, keep us this day from sin. Have mercy on us. O Lord, have mercy on us. Let thy mercy, Lord, be upon us, for we have hoped in Thee. O Lord, in Thee have I trusted, never let me be confounded. Amen.

18

Trust in Providence Brings Peace

The Apostle Paul tells us what we must do, if we will enjoy peace. Very few of us have as many difficulties in life as Paul, yet he was always at peace. Stoned, beaten, left for dead, shipwrecked, arrested, imprisoned, faced with great legal battles in the courts of law, and finally martyred for his faith in Jesus Christ, Paul radiates the peace of God. Here is what he says in his own words:

> Thrice was I beaten with rods, once I was stoned, thrice I suffered shipwreck, a night and a day I was in the depth of the sea. In journeying often, in perils of waters, in perils of robbers, in perils from my own nation, in perils from the Gentiles, in perils in the city, in perils in the wilderness, in perils in the sea, in perils from false brethren. In labor and painfulness, in much watching, in hunger and thirst, in fasting often, in cold and nakedness. Besides those things which are without—my daily instance, the solicitude for all the churches. Who is weak, and I am not weak? Who is scandalized, and I am not on fire? If I must needs glory, I will glory of the things that concern my infirmity. The God and Father of our Lord Jesus Christ, who is blessed for ever, knows that I lie not. (II Co 11:25–31)

Despite all his problems, persecutions, and difficulties, Paul triumphantly proclaims that he has kept the faith in his letter to Timothy, written when he was in prison in Rome, waiting for his martyrdom by the sword. "For I am even now ready to be sacrificed and the time of my dissolution is at hand. I have fought a good fight, I have finished my course, I have kept the faith."

He tells us that he longs to dissolve and be with Christ (Ph 1.23). What is the source of his peace? Absolute trust in the loving Providence of God.

His advice to us is for us not to worry about anything, but by prayer and supplication to make our petitions known to God with thanksgiving. Then the peace of God that surpasses all understanding will keep our hearts and minds in Christ Jesus (Ph 4:6–7).

How do we keep from worrying? By absolute trust in the loving Providence of God. That is the secret of Paul's peace, and it can be ours. Very few of us have had as much that we could worry about as Paul. Yet, he was serene in whatever situation he found himself and constantly blessing people with peace in words such as these: "Now the Lord of peace Himself give you everlasting peace in every place. The Lord be with you all!" (II Th 3:16).

St. Peter also tells us not to worry, but to cast all our care on Jesus, because he takes care of us (I Pe 5:7). Peter learned this the hard way, by denying Jesus at the time of his passion and death. Even though he had been on Mount Tabor and saw Jesus transfigured and glorified, his faith and trust failed him at a crucial time. However, once he saw the Risen Lord, he repented of his lack of faith and trust in Him and gloriously shed his blood by being, traditions tells us, crucified upside down, because he said he was not worthy to die the way Jesus did.

Jesus demands absolute faith and trust in those who follow Him—no matter how dark the way that we must travel. Jesus tells us the same thing He told Paul: "My grace is sufficient for you" (II Co 12:9). Over and over, Jesus tells us not to be afraid. How affectionately and tenderly He phrases it, saying: "Fear not, little flock, for it has pleased your Father to give you a kingdom" (Lk 12:32). Once when the apostles were frightened, He reassured them with these words: "Be of good heart! It is I, fear not!" (Mt 14:27). In all the frightening situations of our lives, we must seek the Lord, knowing that whatever happens to us, He is with us, telling us not to fear. Everything that happens to us is part of God's plan. St. Paul tells us: "We know that to them that love God, all things work together unto good, to such as, according to his purpose, are called to be saints" (Ro 8:28). And that includes all of us—we are all called to be saints. The universal call to holiness is made very clear in the documents of Vatican II. "Therefore all in the Church, whether they belong to the hierarchy or are cared for by it, are called to holiness, according to the apostle's saying: 'For this is the will of God, your sanctification'" (I Th 4:3)(V 39). As if this were not explicit enough, the documents continue: "It is therefore quite clear that all Christians in any state or walk of life are called to the fullness of Christian life and to the perfection of love, and by this holiness a more human manner of life is fostered also in earthly society" (V 41). Our world is enlightened by the presence of the saints of God. As the psalmist says: "God is wonderful in His saints" (66:37). In them we behold glimpses of His beauty.

All things do work together for good for those who love God—even sins—including the sins of other people that are meant to harm us. The enemy intends them to do evil to us, but God turns them around and draws good from them. The greatest evil that the enemy has ever been able to inflict was the death of Jesus on the cross, and by His dying and death He opened heaven to us and made it possible for us to share His very life—the life of grace—by which we participate in the intimate life of God, already in this world, and which prepares us to behold Him in the beatific vision in the life of the world to come.

To get a better understanding of how trust in the Providence of God brings peace to our souls, let us now consider what the eminent Dominican theologian Reginald Garrigou-Lagrange says about it in his monumental work titled *Providence.* We can only single out a few significant thoughts from this very long treatise. If one would like to understand more about Providence, we recommend this book by a master theologian.

Garrigou-Lagrange emphasizes that we do not change God's will or plans with our prayers. Rather with our prayers we participate in God's governance of the world. He foresaw our prayers from all eternity and has willed that we pray them as part of his bringing about His plan. Our prayers are willed by God (205), and our prayers are an act of worship of the Providence of God (207). As we pray, we come to desire what God has desired and willed from all eternity (210). Speaking of Providence he says: "It is *universal,* extending to the minutest detail, to the secrets of the heart. It is *infallible,* regarding everything that happens, even our free actions. *It directs all things to good,* and the prayer of the just will change the heart of the sinner" (173). He points out that Providence permits evil, because it always draws a greater good from it. However, Providence remains in many respects a great mystery. Nevertheless, if we abandon ourselves completely to Providence we will experience peace even in the midst of great difficulties.

According to Garrigou-Lagrange, we should totally abandon ourselves to Divine Providence, because everything that happens has been foreseen by God from all eternity and has been willed or permitted by Him. Secondly, we should abandon ourselves to God's Providence, because nothing can be willed or permitted by Him that does not tend toward His goal in creating—the expression of His perfections and His goodness (217). The third reason we should abandon ourselves to Providence is that all things work together for good for those who love God and are called according to His purpose. (217). However, most importantly, when we abandon ourselves to His Providence, we do not cease from actively trying to do His will that has been expressed to us in the teachings of the Church and in the events of our lives (218). We will benefit greatly from abandoning ourselves to Providence; it will improve our prayer life and draw us into close union with God.

We must abandon everything—the present, the future, and the past. And we must do it "with childlike confidence" (223). Our self-abandonment must be absolute when it concerns events that are independent of our will (227). If we suffer injustice from people, we must bear these injustices with patience. If we find it necessary to retaliate against the injustice because it is an offense to God and/or endangers souls, we should "put ourselves unreservedly in God's hands for the success of the steps we take" (228).

To Garrigou-Lagrange, seeking to do the will of God in the present moment leads to great holiness. We should let the Holy Spirit guide us from moment to moment in all things. He writes: "God is like the ocean, sustaining those who, in all confidence, surrender themselves to Him, and do everything in their power to follow His inspirations, as a ship will respond to a favorable breeze" (250).

God guides those in a special way that abandon themselves to Him bestowing on them all His gifts, especially wisdom and counsel, with everything that happens contributing to their spiritual welfare (250). Garrigou-Lagrange insists that there is no such thing as chance—every little circumstance in this life is controlled by Providence (262). It frequently happens in the lives of the just who abandon themselves to His Providence that special inspirations come to them (263). In addition to His inspirations, He gives these people His grace and the gifts and virtues of the Holy Spirit (265).

God in His Providence foresees that some people are His elect and He loves them more than the others (319). "As for the elect, He sees to it that they continue to observe His precepts until the end (319). Garrigou-Lagrange comments that the grace of a happy death is a special gift given to the elect (320). Our theologian raises the question as to how we can obtain the grace of a happy death. Only God's mercy preserves us from mortal sin and makes it possible for us to persevere. Therefore we should be very humble (326). Although we cannot merit the gift of final perseverance, we can obtain it though prayer by appealing to God's mercy (328). Our theologian then raises the question whether prayer infallibly obtains for us the grace of a happy death. He answers by saying that theology teaches that prayer is infallible under certain conditions—we must ourselves ask for the things we require for salvation, and we must ask with piety and perseverance (320). We must also pray in the name of Jesus, as He has directed us to do. So let us abandon ourselves to God and His Loving Providence and trust His mercy to protect and guide us. Garrigou-Lagrange tells us:

> In this self-abandonment we shall find peace. As our Lord hung dying for us, He experienced in His holy soul the keenest suffering our sins had caused, yet likewise the profoundest peace. So, too, in every Christian death, as in that of the good thief, there is suffering, a holy fear and trembling before the infinite justice of God, and a profound peace, a most intimate union prevailing

between them. Nevertheless it is peace, the tranquility that comes of true order, which predominates, as is apparent from these words of our Lord as He died: 'It is consummated…Father, into Thy hands I commend My spirit' (Luke 23:46).

"Lord, we will try to imitate Your self-abandonment to the Providence of the Heavenly Father. With You we say, 'Into Your hands, I commend my spirit.' We know that in Your Loving Providence, you provide everything we need for this life and for the next. Everything that happens to us is willed or permitted by you—that there is no coincidence or chance governing our lives. Everything is planned by you for our spiritual welfare and happiness. We desire the peace that the world cannot give. We know that peace comes when we abandon our lives into Your hands.

We do so at this very moment, knowing that you care for us far more than we can even dream or imagine. We are safe in Your Hands. Take us in Your holy hands and hold us close to Your heart that Your love may flow into us and transform us. We thank You for Your gift of peace. We will treasure it and try to pass it on to all we encounter. In Your holy name, we pray, Jesus, asking the Heavenly Father to hear us in unity with the Holy Spirit. Amen."

19

Heavenly Peace

Our God is a God of peace and the peace that we shall enjoy, when we behold Him face to face, will be eternal and nothing will be able to disturb it in any way. St. Augustine wrote about this peace in *The City of God*. He tells us that we will forget all our past ills, because we shall have so completely escaped them all, that we will not even remember them. We shall enter into a great Sabbath that has no evening. "We shall ourselves be the seventh day, when we shall be filled and replenished with God's blessing and sanctification." He will completely sanctify us and our "knowledge shall be perfected when we shall be perfectly at rest, and shall perfectly know that He is God. Following this seventh day there will be:

> An eighth and eternal day, consecrated by the resurrection of Christ, and pre-figuring the eternal repose not only of the spirit, but also of the body. There we shall rest and see, see and love, love and praise. This is what shall be in the end without end. For what other end do we propose to ourselves than to attain to the kingdom of which there is no end? (XXII: 29–30)

Before we enter fully into the kingdom, death, the last enemy, must be con-quered. If we live in His grace, we participate in the death and resurrection of Jesus. As St. Paul says, our citizenship is already in heaven. Because we are nur-tured on His Body and Blood, His life courses through us. However, our peace will not be complete until resurrection day, when our bodies are reunited with our souls. We are composed of body and soul. We are not bodies that have souls, or souls that have bodies. We are both body and soul, and we will not be com-plete until they are reunited. St. Bernard describes the yearning that the disem-bodied soul experiences for being reunited with its body.

> It is not in dispute that they want their bodies back; if they thus desire and hope for them, it is clear that they have not wholly turned from themselves, for it is evident that they are still clinging to something which is their own,

even if their desires return to it only a very little. Until death is swallowed up in victory (I Co 15:54), and the everlasting light invades the farthest bounds of night and shines everywhere—so that heavenly glory gleams even in bodies—these souls cannot wholly remove themselves and transport themselves to God. They are still too much bound to their bodies, if not in life and feeling, certainly in natural affection. They do not wish to be complete without them, an indeed they cannot" (*On Loving God* 197)

Our souls will be reunited with our bodies, and St. Augustine assures us that our glorified bodies will be beautiful and compete. If we have a deformity in this life, our bodies will be perfect in the next. We will then also be in the prime of life—about thirty years of age. Augustine also believes that those who died in childhood will rise with adult bodies. Women will be glorified women and men, glorified men, and they will complement each other for all eternity. Being created in the image and likeness of God, they will reflect both the masculine and the feminine attributes of the Creator. For the present, we behold a most beautiful portrayal of God's feminine characteristics in the Mother of Jesus. God's masculine attributes are seen in the life and actions of our Lord Jesus Christ. Together, male and female, we shall reflect the glory of God for each other.

St. Augustine also speaks of the new creation, based on what St. Paul tells us about it that all creation groans waiting for its redemption in Christ.

For the expectation of the creature waits for the revelation of the sons of God. For the creature was made subject to vanity, not willingly, but by reason of him that made it subject, in hope: Because the creature also itself shall be delivered from the servitude of corruption, into the liberty of the glory of the children of God. For we know that every creature groans and travails in pain, even till now. And not only it, but ourselves also, who have the first fruits of the Spirit, even we ourselves groan within ourselves, waiting for the adoption of the sons of God, the redemption of our body. (Ro 8: 19–23)

Holy Scripture assures us that we will have new heavens and a new earth. St. Peter also tells us this. "According to His promise we wait for new heavens and a new earth (II Pe 3:13). St. John in his vision on Patmos saw the New Jerusalem and wrote about it in the book of Revelation. "And I, John, saw the holy city, the new Jerusalem, coming down out of heaven from God, prepared as a bride adorned for her husband" (Re 21:2) In his vision, he beheld the Risen Lord Whose voice was as the sound of many waters. This recalls what the psalmist says about the voice of the Lord.

The voice of the Lord is upon the waters; the God of majesty has thundered. The Lord is upon many waters. The voice of the Lord is in power; the voice of the Lord in magnificence.

The voice of the Lord breaks the cedars: Yes, the Lord shall break the cedars of Libanus and shall reduce them to pieces.

The voice of the Lord divides the flame of fire. The voice of the Lord shakes the desert of Cades. The voice of the Lord prepares the stags, and He will discover the thick woods, and in His temple all shall speak His glory.

The Lord makes the flood to dwell, and the Lord shall sit king for ever. The Lord will give strength to His people: the Lord will bless His people with peace. (Ps 28:3–10)

St. John describes the vision by depicting the radiance of the Risen Lord, saying that his feet were like brass in a blazing furnace and his eyes as a flame of fire. When he saw Him, John fell at His feet as though he were dead. Jesus laid his hand upon him and told him, "Fear not, I am the First and the Last, and alive, and was dead, and behold I am living for ever and ever, and have the keys of death and of hell" (Re 1:14–18).

Writing in the eleventh century, St. Symeon, the New Theologian, abbot of the monastery of St. Mamas in Constantinople, tells us that creation will be transformed from corruption to incorruption, "changed, and then together with it and at the same time, the corrupted bodies of men will be renewed such that man may have an incorrupt, and spiritual, and everlasting country in which to make his home" (35). Explaining that just as we are tried by fire, all creation shall be renewed by fire, St. Symeon says that as a craftsman takes an old copper vessel and puts it in the fire and forges it into a new pot, God will reforge all of creation (36). When creation is reforged it will no longer be the same as it was originally, but will be completely spiritual and immutable (38). It will be, the saint insists, a world that is spiritual and beyond our perception. This is in conformity with what St. Paul says that we will be "sown a physical body" and raised in the resurrection "a spiritual body" (I Co 15:44). According to St. Symeon, the earth will be more beautiful with "an inexpressible beauty, an unfading verdure, ornamented by shining flowers, varied and spiritual" (41). The righteous will inherit this earth. Speaking of them St Symeon says:

If even the hairs of our head are numbered by God who knows all things, then how much more are not we? So all the saints are known long beforehand by God, are at once fore-ordained and numbered, as well as enrolled by name in heaven, and are both members of Christ and called to become one body with him. (51–52)

Christian writers, ancient and modern, have many interesting things to tell us about heaven. Gregory of Nyssa (d ca 386) assures us that if we excel in goodness and holiness, we shall "pass automatically and without effort from this earthly life to the life of Heaven" (*The Lord's Prayer: The Beatitudes* 42). We should, he explains, always keep our eyes on the beauty of the Father and imitate Him (44). The life of heaven is pure and passionless, pure from all evil, and rooted in the will of God (62). Citing the beatitudes, Gregory remarks that the pure in heart shall see God in great blessedness.

> The man who sees God, possesses in this act of seeing, all there is of the things that are good. By this we understand life without end, eternal incorruption, and undying beatitude. With these shall we enjoy the everlasting Kingdom of unceasing happiness; we shall see the true Light and hear the sweet voice of the Spirit; we shall exult perpetually in all that is good in the inaccessible glory." (144)

The peace we shall experience in heaven will contribute to our beatitude. We will be in perfect peace because body and soul will be in perfect harmony and we will be truly the children of God.

St. Francis de Sales (1567–1622), Doctor of the universal Church, in his *Treatise on the Love of God* speaks of the glories of heaven and what it will be like to dwell there.

> But when having arrived in the heavenly Jerusalem, we shall see the great Solomon, the King of Glory, seated upon the throne of His wisdom, manifesting by an incomprehensible brightness the wonders and eternal secrets of His sovereign truth, with such light that our understanding will actually see what it had believed here below—Ah! Then, dearest Theotimus, what raptures! What ecstasies! What love! What sweetness! No, never (shall we say in this excess of sweetness) never could we have conceived that we should see truths so delightsome. We believed indeed all the glorious things that were said of thee, *O great city of God*, but we could not conceive the infinite greatness of the abysses of thy delights." (152–153)

When a soul is plunged into the Divine essence in heaven, St. Francis de Sales says that God will infuse it with the light of glory, "which will enlighten it in this abyss of inaccessible light, so that by the light of glory we may see the light of Divinity" (162). The intensity of our beatitude will depend on the measure we receive of the light of glory. Depending on how much of it we receive, we will behold God more clearly or less so. Greater glory will be the portion of those who receive more of the light of glory. The blessed will swim like fishes in the Divine Ocean of God which will always be infinitely greater than they (164). Our beatitude will never end. Holy Scripture makes that crystal clear. In the book of Daniel we read:

> But in the days of those kingdoms, the God of heaven will set up a kingdom that shall never be destroyed, and His kingdom shall not be delivered up to another people, and it shall break in pieces, and shall consume all these kingdoms, and itself shall stand forever." (2:44)

In our heavenly Jerusalem, God will dwell with men and will wipe away every tear (Rev 21:3–5). There will be no more death, pain, sorrow, or separation from those we love.

From the book of Wisdom, we learn much about the life of the blessed in heaven. It says:

> The souls of the just are in the hand of God, and the torment of death shall not touch them. In the sight of the unwise they seemed to die, and their departure was taken for misery, and their going away from us, for utter destruction, but they are in peace. And though in the sight of men they suffered torments, their hope is full of immortality. Afflicted in few things, in many they shall be well rewarded, because God hath tried them, and found them worthy of Himself. As gold in the furnace, He has proved them, and as a victim of a holocaust, he has received them, and in time there shall be respect had to them. The just shall shine, and shall run to and fro like sparks among the reeds They shall judge nations, and rule over people, and their Lord shall reign for ever. They that trust in Him shall understand the truth, and they that are faithful in love shall rest in Him, for grace and peace is to his elect. (3:1–9)

Our life in heaven, while filled with God's peace, will not be an inactive existence. Rather we shall judge nations and rule over people. Furthermore, we shall be like Him, because we shall see Him as He is (I Jn 3:2).

Basing his theology on St. Thomas Aquinas, the Domincan theologian, Reginald Garrrigou-Lagrange, describes the full flowering of the life of grace in those who experience the beatific vision. We will have an immediate vision of the Divine Essence and will see God better than we can see people in this life with our human eyes. By grace we will participate in His Essence and Life and see Him as He sees Himself, and love Him as He loves Himself, and live by Him forever (*Three Ages* II 646). We will behold the divine perfections, and how His mercy and His justice complement each other. We shall see the Three Persons of the Trinity.

> From all eternity God has an only Son to whom He communicates all His divine nature; He gives Him to be "God of God, light of light." He has willed to have other sons, adopted ones, to whom He communicates a participation in His nature, sanctifying grace in the essence of their souls, and from this grace proceed in their higher faculties the light of glory and charity. Thus, St, Thomas says, 'by the incarnation of the Son we receive adoptive sonship in the likeness of His natural sonship." (647)

The blessed in glory will live in uninterrupted transforming union with God that absolutely nothing can ever diminish. Likewise the love of the blessed will never be diminished. "This love will be sovereignly spontaneous, but no longer free; it will be superior to liberty, ravished by the sovereign Good" (647). Garrigou-Lagrange thinks that we can get some idea of the life of the blessed in heaven by considering the great amount of grace and favors we receive through the intercessions of the saints.

Our beatitude will consist in "the immediate vision of God" (*Life* 220). "In heaven our knowledge will no longer be imperfect; it will be purely intuitive, higher than any created idea. Beatific love will flow necessarily from the vision. This beatific love is not free. It is something higher than liberty (*Life* 220).

While our essential beatitude consists in the vision of God and the beatific love that flows from seeing Him, we will also have accidental beatitude, which we will find in the society of our friends (*Life* 247). The love that we begin on earth with our friends will continue in eternity. According to Garrigou-Lagrange:

> Seeing one another in God, the saints love one another. The degree of this love is measured by nearness to God. Each rejoices in the degree of beatitude which others have received. Yet each loves with special attention those to whom he has been united on earth. (*Life* 244–245)

According to this theologian, the saints live in "intimate unity," the highest intensity with the deepest response, and they are "overflowing with life" (245).

Commenting on the life of the blessed in heaven, St. Cyprian (martyred 258) writes:

> What glory and what joy to be admitted to see God, to be honored with Christ our Lord! This is the joy of salvation; this is eternal life—to live with the just, with all the friends of God in the kingdom of immortality. When

God shall shine upon us, we will rejoice with inexpressible gladness, sharing forever the kingdom of Christ." (Ep LVI)

By far and away the most exciting and satisfying depiction of the life of the blessed is that of St. Gregory of Nyssa (b ca. 330). In his view, we shall be "transformed from glory to glory," as St. Paul says (II Co 3:28). According to Gregory, although St. Paul had wonderful visions of heaven, he forgets what is past and reaches for what is still be attained. Here are Paul's words.

> Brethren, I do not count myself to have apprehended. But one thing I do, forgetting the things that are behind, and stretching forth myself to those that are before, I press towards the mark, to the prize of the supernal vocation of God in Christ Jesus. Let us therefore, as many as are perfect, be thus minded; and if in anything you be otherwise minded, this also God will reveal to you. (Ph 3:13–15)

Commenting on this statement from Paul, Gregory says, "Thus, he teaches us, I think, that in our constant participation in the blessed nature of the Good, the graces that we receive at every point are indeed great, but the path that lies beyond our immediate grasp is infinite" (*From Glory* 211–212). For this reason, he believes that the blessed in glory "will always enjoy a greater and greater participation in grace throughout all eternity (212). To substantiate the idea that we shall grow in grace eternally, he points out that Moses, after having been allowed to speak with God face to face, had an insatiable desire for more of Him (*From Glory* 263).

> Thus though the new grace we may obtain is greater than what we had before, it does not put a limit on our final goal, rather, for those who are rising in perfection, the limit of the good that is attained becomes the beginning of the discovery of higher goods. Thus they never stop rising, moving from one new beginning to the next, and the beginning of ever greater graces is never limited of itself. For the desire of those who thus rise never rests in what they can already understand; but by an ever greater and greater desire, the soul keeps rising constantly to another which lies ahead, and thus it makes its way through ever higher regions towards the Transcendent. (*From Glory* 212–213)

Our future is glorious. Our essential beatitude, if we are faithful and persevere, is the vision of God, and if, Gregory of Nyssa is correct, we will always continue to penetrate ever more deeply into the mystery of the Trinity. Our joy will be full of glory and will never end. We will share most intimately in the life of God forever and ever.

We must remember that we are an ecclesial community and that in heaven we will enjoy, as our accidental beatitude, the companionship of those we love. We will be able to love each other to degrees unknown in this life. We will be able to receive the tremendous outpouring of love from all the saints of God—everyone in heaven will be a saint and will love us. Great love will flow between us and those we knew and loved in this life, and we will never be separated from them again. We will rejoice at seeing those we have loved on earth filled with the light of glory and ecstatic with the love of God. Death, the last enemy, will have been conquered and God will be All in all. Peace, heavenly peace, will flow from one end of heaven to the other and we will all be caught up in the embrace of God.

Note

All Bible quotations are from the Douay-Rheims edition that is in the public domain. We have replaced the archaic verb forms and pronouns with ones consistent with modern usage. The Douay-Rheims Bible can be found at http://www.gutenberg.org.

Works Cited

Anselm of Canterbury. *De Casu Diaboli.* http://romancatholicism.org/anselm-works.htm.

Ambrose, St. *De Mysteriis.* www.ldysinger.com/MONS_423/05_lit-prayer/03_ambrose.htm.

_____. *Holy Spirit.* www.newadvent.org/fathers/34021.htm.

Augustine, *St. Confessions.* www.stoa.org/hippo.

_____. *City of God.* www.ccel.org/fathers/NPNF1–02.

_____. Letter 98 to Bishop Boniface. www.ccel.org/fathers/NPNF1–01.

_____. Sermon LXXXI. http://www.ccel.org/fathers2/NPNF1–06/npnf1–06–98.htm#P6261_2651478.

Basil the Great, St. *De Spiritu Sancto.* http://www.newadvent.org/fathers/3201000.htm.

Bernard of Clairvaux. *Selected Works.* Trans. G.R. Evans. Paulist Press: NY, 1987.

Cassian, John. *Conferences.* www.osb.org/lectio/cassian/conf .

Catechism of the Catholic Church. Liberaia Editrice: Vatican, 1994.

Council of Trent. http://history.hanover.edu/early/trent.htm

Conger, Yves. *I Believe in the Holy Spirit.* Trans. David Smith. Crossroad: New York, 1983.

Cyprian of Carthage. Ep LVI ad Thibaritanos, 10 (Journel, no 579) quoted in Garrigou-Lagrange. *Life Everlasting.*

Cyril of Jerusalem. *Catechetical Lectures*. www.ocf.org/OrthodoxPage/reading/ St.Pachomius.

Dante Alighieri. *Divine Comedy*. Trans. Longfellow. http://www.gutenberg.org/ etext/1004.

Didache: Or the Teaching of the Twelve Apostles. www.ocf.org/OrthodoxPage/ reading/St.Pachomius.

Francis de Sales. *Treatise on the Love of God*. Trans. Henry Benedict Mackey, O.S.B. Tan Books: Rockford, Illinois, 1997.

Garrigou Lagrange, Reginald, O.P. *Life Everlasting*. TAN: Rockford, IL, 1991.

_____. Providence. Tan: Rockford, IL. 1998.

_____. *The Three Ages of the Interior Life: Prelude of Eternal Life*. Trans. Sister M Timothea Doyle, O.P. B. Herder: St. Louis, MO, 1948.

Gregory of Nyssa. *From Glory to Glory: Texts from Gregory of Nyssa's Mystical Writings*. Trans and Ed. Herbert Musurillo, S.J. Scribners: New York, 1961.

_____. *The Great Catechism.* http://www.ccel.org/fathers2/NPNF2–05/Npnf2– 05–39.htm.

_____. *The Lord's Prayer: The Beatitudes*. Trans. Hilda Graef. Paulist Press: NY, 1954.

Hilary of Poitiers. *De Trinitate*.. http://www.ccel.org/fathers2/NPNF2–09/ Npnf2–09–15.htm.

Irenaeus, St. *Adversus Haereses*. http://www.ccel.org/fathers2/ANF-01/anf01– 56.htm.

Jerome, St. *De viris illustribus*. http://www.newadvent.org/fathers/2708.htm.

John Chrysostom, St. *Divine Liturgy*. www.ocf.org/OrthodoxPage/liturgy/ liturgy.html.

_____. *Homilies*. www.ccel.org/fathers and www.newadvent.org/fathers/ 2001.htm.

_____."No One Can Harm the Man Who Does Not Harm Himself." www.newadvent.org/fathers/1902.htm.

_____. *On the Priesthood.* http://www.ccel.org/fathers2/NPNF1–09/TOC.htm.

John of Damascus, St. *Writings.* Trans. Frederic H. Chase, Jr. Fathers of the Church: New York, 1958.

John Paul II. *Dominum et Vivificantum,* May 18, 1986, www.vatican.va/edocs/ENG0142/_INDEX.HTM.

_____. Homily San Antonio. Texas. September 13, 1987.

_____. "Reconciliation and Penance." www.vatican.va/holy_father/john_paul_ii/apost_exhortations/.

Justin Martyr, St. *Dialog with Trypho.* www.angelfire.com/yt3/mxx/dialogugetrypho.htm.

_____. First Apology. http://www.ccel.org/fathers.

Leo XIII. *Divinum Illud Munu.* May 9, 1897. www.vatican.va/holy_father/leo_xiii.

Martyrdom of Ignatius. http://www.newadvent.org/fathers/0123.htm.

Origen, *Against Celsus.* http://www.ccel.org/fathers2/ANF-04/anf04–55.htm.

_____. Homilies on Numbers. www.bringyou.to/apologetics/num8.htm.

Paul VI. *Gaudium et Spes.* December 7, 1965. ww.vatican.va/jubilee_2000/magazine/documents.

Pius XII. Radio Message to the U.S. National Catechetical Congress in Boston (October 26,1946): Discorsi e Radiomessaggi VIII (1946).

Shakespeare, William. *King Henry the Sixth.* http://www.gutenberg.net/etext/1765.

Symeon. St. . *On the Mystical Life: Ethical Discourses.* Vol 1. Trans. Alexander Golitzin. St. Vladimir's Seminary Press: Crestwood, NY, 1995.

Tertullian. *On the Resurrection of the Flesh*. *http://www.newadvent.org/fathers/0316.htm*.

Thomas a Kempis. *Imitation of Christ*. Project Gutenberg.

St. Thomas Aquinas. *Commentum in Joannem*. 4.3.

_____. Summa Theologica. http://www.newadvent.org/summa/.

Vatican Council II: The Conciliar and Post Conciliar Documents. Austin Flannery, O.P. Ed. St Paul's Editions: Boston, MA 1975.

Vianney, John-Baptiste-Marie. *Sermons*.www.theworkofgod.org/Library/Sermons/JdVianey/Sermons.htm.

Wilde, Oscar. "Ballad of Reading Gaol." http://www.gutenberg.net/dirs/etext95/rgaol10.txt.

About the Authors

Ricardo C. Castellanos, L. S, T.

Born in Camaguez, Cuba in 1945, Rev. Ricardo C. Castellanos came to the United States in 1961. He received a B.A. degree in philosophy from the Granada Dominican College in Granada, Spain. From the Gregorian University in Rome, he received his L.S.T. degree in theology and was ordained May 17, 1970 in St. Peters Basilica in Rome by Pope Paul VI. He has lectured extensively on motivational topics on television and radio in the United States, Europe, South America, and in outreach ministry to the Middle East and Japan. He is author of countless motivational audio and video materials in both Spanish and English, including *Attacks on the Family, Ten Steps to Refresh Your Marriage, The Family, Anger and Pardon, Interior Healing, Steps in Christian Family Living, El Camino del Gozo, No tengas miedo, Pasos para Sanar Nuestra Imagen, Los Angeles y los Demonios*, among countless others. He is coauthor with Allienne R. Becker of *All You Need is Love: The Way of Joy* and *Be Free! The Gift of Freedom*, IUnivers 2003. To learn more about these materials visit the website www.beckerinprint.com. A forthcoming book on faith is to be published by Ricardo Castellanos and Allienne Becker in 2005.

Allienne R. Becker Ph. D.

Dr. Allienne R. Becker has a B. A. degree from Duke University, two M.A. degrees from West Virginia University, and a Ph.D. from the Pennsylvania State University. She is an emerita of the State System of Higher Education for the Commonwealth of Pennsylvania, having taught at Lock Haven University for twenty-seven years and is the author of several academic books published by Greenwood Press. Her interest in religion and hagiography let her to publishing *I, Paul...: The Life of the Apostle to the Gentiles*, Writers Club Press, 2001 and *Eagle in Flight: The Life of Athanasius, the Apostle of the Trinity*, Writers Club Press, 2002. She is coauthor with Ricardo C. Castellanos of *All You Need is Love: The Way of Joy* and *Be Free! The Gift of Freedom*, Writers Club Press, 2003. They are working on a forthcoming book on faith to be published in 2005. Visit the website www.beckerinprint.com to learn more about her publications.

0-595-33905-0